The Book of the
PRINCESS ROYAL PACIFICS

A British Railways Illustrated Special

By Ian Sixsmith
With additional notes by Graham Onley

IRWELL PRESS

Copyright IRWELL PRESS
ISBN 1-903266-01-7
First published in the United Kingdom in 2000
by Irwell Press
59A, High Street, Clophill,
Bedfordshire MK45 4BE
Printed by The Amadeus Press

Acknowledgements

Little that is *wholly* new remains to be said concerning any major class of British steam locomotive, though of course there is still a lot to celebrate and illustrate. A similar point was made in the three preceding books of this series – *The Book of the BR Standards*, *The Book of the Coronation Pacifics* and *The Book of the Royal Scots*. There are always a few nuggets to be had, and one or two particularly glistening ones, I like to think, have been introduced to the story of the Princess Royals. The complete Engine Record is again something rather new. For the great part, the photographs have not been seen before and my special thanks go to Barry Hoper for help in this regard. I couldn't get away without thanking Janet too, while a mention of Jamie might help steer him towards new century railway enthusiasm. Will he ever thank us we wonder?

Many thanks go once again to Allan Baker, Stephen Summerson, Alec Swain, Martin Smith, Geoff Goslin and Eric Youldon, and I must especially thank Peter Rowledge. John Jennison of Brassmasters (purveyors to the gentry of fine etched brass LMS locomotive kits) once again very kindly made available copies of the Record Cards.

Bibliography

The Locomotive, The Railway Engineer, LMS Magazine, BR London Midland Magazine, The Railway Gazette, The Railway Observer, Journal of the Stephenson Locomotive Society, various record series at Kew – principally RAIL 418, 422, *The LMS Pacifics* (Rowledge, D&C, 1987), *Loco Profile – LMS Pacifics* (Reed, Profile Publications 1974), *British Pacific Locomotives* (Allen, Ian Allan, 1962), *An Illustrated History of LMS Locomotives* (Essery and Jenkinson, SLP 1989), *London Midland Fireman* (Higson, Ian Allan 1972), *LMS Locomotive Names* (RCTS 1994) and various issues of all sorts of magazines.

Cover: **46203 PRINCESS MARGARET ROSE at Polmadie shed, 4 November 1951. Photograph J.L. Stevenson.**
Below: **46201 PRINCESS ELIZABETH at Polmadie in August 1953. Photograph J.L. Stevenson.**

Contents

THE PRINCESS ROYAL at Camden – note how the lining is 'carried round' the tender front in a 'mini' panel of its own. It was stationed at the London shed throughout the 1930s; a sign of the times is the L&Y type 4-6-0 in the background, which suggests a Cup Final Day or some other special occasion. After that could hardly be found at one shed for much more than a year at a time. The Davies & Metcalfe exhaust steam injector, detailed by *The Railway Gazette* and other contemporary journals, drips water under the cab. Sanding was by simple gravity feed to the front of the leading coupled wheel and the front and back of the intermediate wheel. On the first Pacifics there was an odd system; at the rear of the trailing wheel (clearly visible here) was another tube – not a sander but a water jet, to clean the rails with hot water after sanding and prevent interference with track circuits. The very reverse seems to have been the case; the water device was done away with and, later on, steam sanding substituted. Photograph P. Ransome-Wallis.

AN LMS PACIFIC

'To sum up, we regard the engine as something of which not only Mr. Stanier and his staffs at Derby and Crewe, but also the railway company and directors, may be justly proud.' **The Railway Gazette, 30 June 1933.**

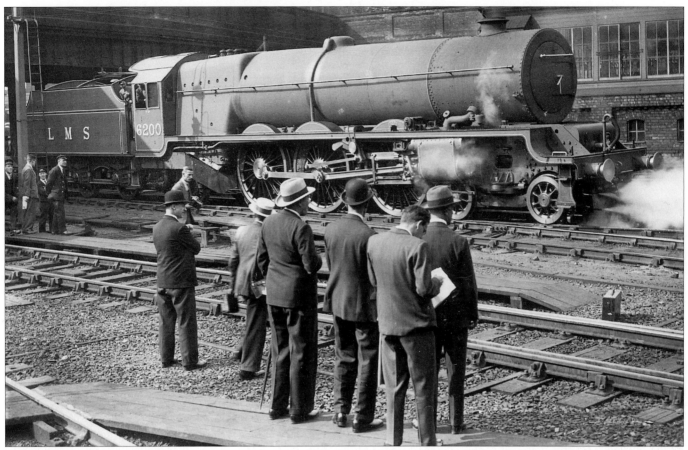

28 June 1933, 6200 had been shown at Euston, nameless and in grey, and this remarkable photograph captures that very day. Note the shiny wheels and motion, absence of smokebox number plate and the *round* buffers. The posse of hats, in various styles, presumably denote a good slice of the LMS Board.

William Stanier's appointment to the LMS as Chief Mechanical Engineer was announced at the end of 1931, and with this began an era in steam design and building that only came to a close, in effect, with the abandonment of steam development by BR in the middle 1950s. The background and the circumstances of Stanier's accession to the LMS are well known and have been described many times, not least in the preceding volumes to this work, *The Book of the Coronation Pacifics* and *The Book of the Royal Scots*, both published by Irwell Press.

The situation that Stanier faced has also been documented at considerable length; it was 'truly appalling' to its despairing Directors and, to wags outside, LMS stood for 'ell of a mess'. George Hughes had become CME when the L&Y and the LNWR came together in 1922 (maybe in an attempt, among other things, to head off a Midland take-over – though there is no evidence to support such a notion). The Grouping came a year later and at first the signs were good, for Hughes knew all about standardisation and was aware of the new, giant, company's future needs. A new scheme of twelve locomotives to meet every need was soon in existence. In the event only the 5ft.6in. 'Crab' was to appear, in May 1926, months after Hughes had retired. From

now on Derby was in charge but as the 1930s dawned and the country found itself in economic mire, LMS locomotive stock, apart from the Royal Scots, was indeed in *'ell of a mess.*

Stanier was appointed from 1 January 1932 following some fairly cloak and dagger meetings with his future employers at various London clubs – the best account remains H.A.V. Bulleid's in his *Master Builders of Steam* (Ian Allan, 1963). Sir Harold Hartley of the LMS spoke with Stanier, together with Sir Ernest Lemon, the 'caretaker' CME after Fowler's departure. *'Stanier was the man'* Hartley said, *'to get our locomotive programme straightened out. The number of different types we had inherited was appalling...'*

A Pacific had been on the cards from the first days of the LMS – Cox had drawn one out in 1924 and Fowler afterwards came up with plans for a compound 4-6-2. Stanier's first locomotive was a 2-6-0, a Crab (in operating, not mechanical terms) to which the taper boiler and other new features of the New Order had been applied. Yet it could not be long before the new CME came up with the next generation of top-flight express power, the touchstone by which his regime would be judged. A year and half into his time on the LMS, Stanier produced the long-awaited Pacific.

6200 THE PRINCESS ROYAL

Work on the new project had begun once Stanier arrived, and consideration was given to both four and three cylinder layout. This new engine obviously had to set the main schedules alight, or at least warm them through thoroughly; this meant Euston-Glasgow, with the biggest passenger trains. Three Pacifics were planned in the first instance, yet they were but small part of the revolution under way; this is clear from the Locomotive Renewal Programme for 1933, presented to the Mechanical & Electrical Engineering Committee on 27 July 1932:

'Submitted, with the approval of the Executive Committee, a Report from the Chief Mechanical Engineer, the Chief General Superintendent and the Chief Accountant regarding the locomotive renewal programme for 1933.

'In a review of the short term programme authorised for 1932, the completion of which was to coincide with the Company's financial year, the report explained that the work of building the 75 new locomotives and the breaking up of the 172 engines was proceeding according to programme, with the exception that as a result of experience gained with the No.7 0-8-0 standard freight tender engine, it was considered that material advantages in reliability and haulage capacity

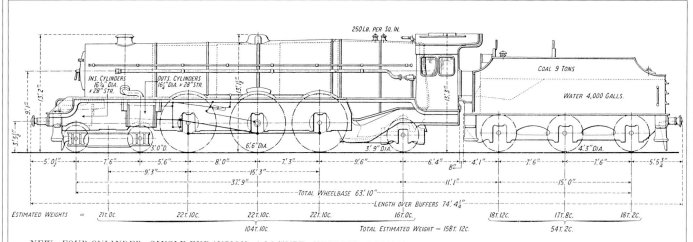

250 LB. PER SQ. IN.

INS. CYLINDERS 16¼ DIA. x 28" STR.
OUTS. CYLINDERS 16¼" DIA. x 28" STR.

COAL 9 TONS
WATER 4,000 GALLS.

13'.2"
9'.1½"
3'.5½"
15'.1½"
13'.3"
3'.0"D
6'.6" DIA.
3'.9" DIA.
4'.3" DIA.

5'.0½" — 7'.6" — 5'.6" — 8'.0" — 7'.3" — 9'.6" — 6'.4" — 8" — 4'.1" — 7'.6" — 7'.6" — 5'.5¾"
9'.3" — 15'.3"
37'.9" — 11'.1" — 15'.0"
TOTAL WHEELBASE 63'.10"
LENGTH OVER BUFFERS 74'.4¼"

ESTIMATED WEIGHTS = 21T. 0C. 22T. 10C. 22T. 10C. 22T. 10C. 16T. 0C. 18T. 12C. 17T. 8C. 18T. 2C.
104T. 10C. TOTAL ESTIMATED WEIGHT = 158T. 12C. 54T. 2C.

NEW FOUR-CYLINDER SINGLE-EXPANSION 4-6-2-TYPE EXPRESS LOCOMOTIVE, LONDON MIDLAND & SCOTTISH RAILWAY

Designed at Derby, built at Crewe.   W. A. Stanier, Chief Mechanical Engineer

THE RAILWAY GAZETTE   June 30, 1933

would be obtained by introducing as a standard a locomotive of the 2-8-0 type, instead of the present 0-8-0, and with this object in view only 15 of the twenty 0-8-0 engines authorised in the 1932 programme were being built, the remaining five being included as 2-8-0 engines in the 1933 programme.

'The estimated cost of £97,695 authorised would therefore be reduced by £24,425 to £73,270 so far as the 1932 programme was concerned.

'In addition, it was considered that, in view of the work to be performed by the five 0-4-0 saturated freight tank engines authorised at a cost of £12,220 in the 1932 programme, a simple saddle tank engine, of the type built for colliery and works purposes, would meet requirements, and in anticipation of the approval of the Directors the tender of Messrs. Kitson of Leeds, amounting to £7,379, had been accepted for five saddle tank engines.

'The total estimated cost of the 1932 programme would therefore be reduced by £29,266 in respect of these two variations, to £315,088.

'Consideration had been given to the 1933 requirements in order to maintain the economic continuity of new work in the Company's workshops, and having regard to the elimination of old and uneconomic types of locomotives, and the standardisation of the Company's stock, it was recommended that during 1933 the following 128 new locomotives be constructed in the Company's workshops at a total estimated cost of £741,435, including the five 2-8-0 freight tender engines referred to, and the fifteen new tenders authorised by Traffic Committee Minute No.3000 and Mechanical and Electrical Engineering Committee Minute No.19 of January 1932 in connection with the conversion of fifteen 'Claughton' engines from four to three cylinders. The details are given in the following table. [see table opposite].

6200 THE PRINCESS ROYAL, without smokebox number plate. This is the official photograph, taken at Crewe to show off the new engine. Note the early provision of vacuum pump, driven by a lever off the crosshead. These were withdrawn from 1938, for they were unreliable and expensive to maintain; a 'small' vacuum ejector served after that. 6200 had been put on show at Euston in grey and without a name, though when it entered service it carried plates which just read PRINCESS ROYAL. Little more than a week later it went back to Crewe for this picture with the definite article added, after which it got the crimson lake livery. Note complex tender axlebox covers – indicating the roller bearings which were fitted to the first two – and also the 'trickle' sanding (it could equally well be termed 'gravity' or 'mechanical'). Steam sanding was fitted as a later 'mod'.

Description	No.	Engines	Estimated Cost Tenders	Total
PASS. TENDER				
4-6-2 Superheated	3	£24,225	£3,405	£27,630
4-6-0 Superheated Converted Claughtons	25	£124,500	£22,500	£165,000
4-6-0 Superheated Converted Prince of Wales	10	£56,000	£9,000	£65,000
Total Passenger	38	£222,725	£34,905	£257,630
FREIGHT TENDER				
2-8-0 Superheated	5	£27,000	£4,500	£31,500
2-6-0 Superheated, Mixed	40	£172,000	£36,000	£208,000
Total Freight	45	£199,000	£40,500	£239,500
PASSENGER TANK				
2-6-4 Superheated	45	£229,500		£229,500
Total Tender Engines	83	£421,725	£75,405	£497,130
Total Tank Engines	45	£229,500		£229,500
Tenders already Authorised	15		£14,805	£14,805
TOTAL Engines	128			
Tenders	98	£651,225	£90,210	£741,435

'The 128 locomotives to be constructed would replace 152 to be broken up, and in addition it was proposed to break up a further 250 engines, a total of 402, at a total replacement cost of £1,295,775

'The breaking up programme would further reduce the number of types of old engines from 252 to 241 and in consequence of the complete elimination of an additional 11 types, certain materials now in stock would become obsolete, the loss under this head being estimated at £2,403

'The estimated charge to the Renewal Fund on the proposed building and breaking up would, after taking into account the loss due to the obsolescence of materials (£2,403) and the scrap value of the locomotives displaced (£51,354) was £692,484, the provision in the 1931 accounts being £718,000.

'Based on the annual mileage, the average cost per engine mile of the new locomotives, as compared with the locomotives to be displaced, would shew an estimated saving of £32,611 per annum, and in addition there would be a further estimated saving of £30,357 per annum in interest at 5½% on the decreased cost of the 128 new engines compared with the estimated replacement cost of the 402 engines to be displaced.

'The Chairman stated that the matter had been recommended to the Board by the Traffic Committee subject to reference to the Mechanical & Electrical Engineering committee.'

Stanier plumped for four cylinders ('because he was used to it' says Bulleid) and because it offered better balancing. With 22½ tons axle weight the new Pacific was heavier than a Royal Scot in this respect by more than a ton and a half, but objections from the Chief Civil Engineer were stilled in the light of the more even hammer blow of such an engine. A Royal Scot's 62½ tons on the six-coupled wheels represented the maximum allowed by the Civil Engineer over existing bridges; a four cylinder engine, with no appreciable hammer blow, could have its weight on the coupled wheels increased by the amount of hammer blow for the three cylinder one, without putting any additional load on the said bridges. Stanier decided the engine would have four cylinders, and the Civil Engineer had to agree that the weight on the coupled wheels should be increased to 67½ tons, with a tractive effort of 40,000lb.

The new engine had many elements that were very 'King'-like – the wheel diameter and cylinder dimensions were precisely the same for instance, along with the boiler pressure and tractive effort. It would be very unwise to emphasise this, for though 6200 was, in some senses, what a Great Western Pacific would have looked like, it nevertheless had many features which set it firmly apart.

Stanier wrote that only a Pacific could overcome the inherent limitations of the Royal Scots. Excellent though they were, the adhesive weight available on the coupled wheels would only allow a sufficient tractive effort for a Royal Scot to take 420 tons unaided from London

Cool and grey, dappled with light inside Crewe North shed, in the few days in June and July 1933 that it ran in 'works' paint. The 15 shedplate picked out by a ray of sunlight was the designation for Crewe North before the recodings of 1935. The nameplate is blank. Photograph Locofotos.

6200 THE PRINCESS ROYAL, now with smokebox plate, after arrival at Euston with the up Royal Scot. It now carries the 1 code for Camden, and is obviously exciting some platform interest. Once the two Pacifics, 6200 and 6201 were both available, the LMS put them to the task envisaged – the oft-stated '500 tons London-Glasgow'. This meant the Royal Scot train, with the crews changing over at Carlisle. Oval buffers have been fitted at the front by now; with such a long locomotive the original ones were found liable to locking when the owner was being shunted around a shed yard – the oval ones obviated the problem.

through to Scotland. The problem was that the Scots, then the biggest LMS express engines, were limited by grate area over continuous runs of more than, say, 300 miles. This in turn limited the power output of the boiler and the period

for which the fire could remain free of clinker. Something more powerful was required, a Pacific with a wide firebox carried behind the frames in order to give the necessary grate area – forty-five square feet.

The design was worked out at Derby and most would agree with *The Railway Engineer* of the time that the result was *'a particularly fine locomotive built on orthodox lines, but incorporating features which cannot in any sense be*

6200, still with its first boiler and tender, photographed at an unrecorded location, but thought to be north of the border – Carstairs probably, from the look of the signals. 6200 carries the curious Caledonian Railway semaphore-style route indicator on the top lamp bracket. A photograph published in Rowledge's *The LMS Pacifics* (D&C, 1987) shows it after arrival at Euston in May 1934, bearing the same CR indicator. Though they remained in use well in to the 1950s (looking decidedly strange on Clans, Britannias, BR 4-6-0s and the like) and in to the 1960s too for all I know, this sort of fixture never made it south of Carlisle much after the 1930s. Photograph W. Hermiston, B.P. Hoper Collection.

As 46200, with LMS still on its 10 ton 'high swept' tender, THE PRINCESS ROYAL comes round the curve at Berkhamsted (betrayed by the chequer pattern board denoting a TPO pick-up) about 1948. The boiler detail changes in the Princess Royal Pacifics are never-ending; it would be tedious to keep referring to them in the captions so the engine picking needs of readers are designed to be catered for in the boiler tables.

called common, and representing a great deal of mature and careful thought and investigation'. THE PRINCESS ROYAL had an independent set of Walshaerts motion for each cylinder, two inside and two outside. This was in contrast to the Kings, where the inside Walshaerts gear operated the valves of the outside cylinders by rocking levers. This, its designer declared, was done with the object of avoiding the inequalities inherent when one piston valve is controlled by means of a lever from the motion of another. The piston valves were 8in. in diameter and had a rather unusual length of travel, 7¼in.. Narrow type piston rings were used, for following their general adoption such an arrangement had given excellent results. The result was reduced wear in the rings and the liners, with a better steam consumption. The outside cylinders were inclined at 1 in 35, but the inside ones were horizontal.

'To provide sufficient boiler power and allow longer runs to be made', Stanier wrote, *'recourse therefore had to be made to a wide firebox carried on top of the frames behind the coupled wheels, and an additional pair of carrying wheels had to be provided for the overhang'*. To run 500

46200 near Shrewsbury with non-corridor stock, on what is surely one of Crewe's filling in jobs, 19 May 1956. Photograph B.P. Hoper Collection.

On a Perth-Euston train at Trimby Grange (north of Shap, between Shap and Eden Valley Junction) on 6 July 1957. Photograph Les Elsey.

46200 THE PRINCESS ROYAL

Built Crewe
LM 'date built' 27 June 1933
Renumbered 6200 to 46200 week ending 14/8/48

REPAIRS	
All Crewe unless	19/10/44-17/11/44**HG** (26)
stated otherwise	22/3/45-21/4/45**LO** (27)
Figure in brackets	26/11/45-1/1/46**HS** (31)
= weekdays out of traffic	4/6/46-29/7/46**HO** (48)
	5/2/47-15/3/47**LS** (34)
30/5/34-12/6/34**LS**	21/7/47-16/9/47**HG** (50)
9/3/35-9/5/35**HS**	4/2/48-5/3/48**LO** (27)
3/6/35-7/6/35**LO**	12/7/48-14/8/48**HS** (30)
13/6/35-21/6/35**HO**	18/2/49-27/5/49**HI** (84)
19/11/35-24/1/36**HO**	28/7/49-22/9/49**HC** (49)
19/4/36-14/5/36**LS**	27/12/49-7/2/50**HO** (36)
27/7/36-30/7/36**LO**	31/5/50-28/7/50**HI** (47)
30/9/36-12/10/36**HO**	15/3/51-19/5/51**HI** (55)
9/11/36-23/11/36**LO**	21/11/51-7/4/52**HG** (116)
21/1/37-10/2/37**LO**(18)	4/11/52-29/11/52**HC** (22)
30/4/37-10/6/37**HG**(36)	17/1/53-16/5/53**HI** (101)
19/5/38-23/6/38**LS** (31)	29/4/54-11/6/54**LI** (37)
29/10/38-21/11/38**LO** (20)	17/9/54-15/10/54**LC(EO)** (24)
8/8/39-9/9/39**HG** (29)	20/7/55-27/8/55**HI(EO)** (33)
26/2/40-20/3/40**LO** (21)	31/8/55-16/9/55**NC(Rect)(EO)** (14)
6/9/40-24/9/40**LS** (16)	25/9/56-8/11/56**HG** (38)
6/3/41-2/4/41**LO** (24)	29/1/57-2/3/57**HC(EO)** (28)
25/9/41-18/10/41**HS** (21)	9/11/57-15/11/57**NC(EO)** (5)
21/4/42-23/6/42**HG** (55)	9/3/58-6/6/58**HI** (67)
1/9/42-19/9/42**LO** (17)	22/9/58-23/10/58**LC(EO)** (27)
30/1/43-2/3/43**LO** (27)	6/11/58-6/12/58**HC(EO)** (26)
16/3/43-1/4/43**LO** (15)	29/4/59-18/6/59**LC(EO)** (43)
4/10/43-4/11/43**LS** (28)	10/9/59-10/9/59**LC** (1) *St Rollox*
18/5/44-17/6/44**LO** (27)	14/12/59-30/1/60**HG** (39)

MILEAGES	
1933	26,781
1934	78,158
1935	47,687
1936	67,464
1937	61,712
1938	72,873
1939	50,076
1940	71,140
1941	53,758
1942	59,373
1943	49,191
1944	53,876
1945	60,244
1946	58,403
1947	52,483
1948	55,942
1949	38,404
1950	61,329
1951	48,449
1952	47,682
1953	51,055
1954	54,773
1955	42,257
1956	52,260
1957	53,140
1958	41,979
1959	58,998
1960	55,144

Mileage at 31/12/50 1,018,894
Mileage at 12/60 1,524,631
Withdrawn week ending 17/11/62
Scrapped J.Connel Ltd,
Coatbridge, 9/64

SHEDS	
Camden	30/9/33
Edge Hill	6/4/42
Camden (loan)	21/3/42
Edge Hill	16/5/42
Camden (loan)	17/10/42
Edge Hill	3/4/43
Crewe North	22/5/43
Edge Hill	20/5/44
Crewe North (loan)	18/10/47
Edge Hill	17/1/48
Crewe North	13/3/48
Edge Hill	11/12/48
Polmadie (loan)	22/9/51
Edge Hill	16/5/53
Crewe North	23/5/53
Edge Hill	11/9/53
Carlisle Upperby	12/6/54
Crewe North	26/6/54
Edge Hill	18/9/54
Crewe North	25/6/55
Edge Hill	15/9/56
Crewe North	22/6/57
Edge Hill	21/9/57
Crewe North	20/6/59
Carnforth	2/9/61
Carlisle Upperby	27/1/62
Carlisle Kingmoor	7/4/62

TENDERS	
No	Fitted
9000	27/6/33
9065	9/5/35
9066	20/6/56
9372	25/11/36
9376	27/8/55

ton trains between London and Glasgow the LMS needed a Pacific, which was of course (if we want to put the whole development story of the Princesses in a single sentence) merely the 'next size up' from a 4-6-0.

Stanier improved the boiler (he didn't think much of the existing parallel Royal Scot one – see *The Book of the Royal Scots*, page 17) and devised a ta-per boiler with much increased grate area, 'to ensure satisfactory combustion during long through runs'. The grate area was intimidating at 45sq.ft., a figure which of itself dictated a wide firebox. Moreover, a grate this size, it was thought, was near to the limit of efficient firing by hand. To carry such a firebox, a specially designed 'Bissel type' trailing truck was provided. Here at the rear end it formed one of the locomotive's most noticeable features – the massively-built extra plates fixed to the main frame and then swept outwards and rearwards right along the base of the firebox, obscuring the springs of the trailing wheels. These were the 'arms' of the truck, and were anchored to a stretcher carried between the main frames. The load on the truck was thus transmitted from the main

46200 roars along at Beattock in the early part of the 1950s; the photographer John Robertson is standing by the telegraph pole, enjoying the wonderful scene. Various alterations took place in the 'chassis' of the Princesses throughout the 1950s; there was the front 'rebuilding' wherein most of them (the ones that needed them) got new front end frames from 1952 to 1954, frame stretchers and axlebox guides were strengthened, bogie springs were improved and various other alterations made. Photograph W. Hermiston, B.P. Hoper Collection.

46200 in Brunswick green, about to pass Shap Summit box with the 11.15am Birmingham New Street to Glasgow express, on Saturday 7 June 1952. Photograph E.D. Bruton.

frames by means of side bolsters. For this to work properly, an arrangement of side control springs was very carefully worked out.

The wide Belpaire firebox was carefully proportioned with great attention to the water circulation around it. The 'water legs' – the areas at the sides between the inner and outer firebox where water had to circulate freely – was 'carefully proportioned' to ensure just

that. Feed water came through top feed clacks, and the boiler on 6200 did not have a steam dome – what looked like the dome was in fact a cover for the top-feed. The superheater header and regulator were combined and fitted in the smokebox; steam was collected not in the 'dome' but GWR-fashion, through a perforated pipe high up in the front of the firebox. From here steam went through a seven inch main pipe to the regulator

and superheater header. The superheater was of a new design, with sixteen elements providing a heating surface of 350sq.ft.. Of this, more anon…

The new engine had four three inch diameter Ross-pop safety valves mounted conventionally on the firebox, while the old Caledonian design of whistle had been revived, to give, *The Railway Gazette* noted approvingly, 'a deep and melodious note'. To satisfy gauge re-

The familiar Platform 1 at Euston, 25 May 1958. THE PRINCESS ROYAL was an Edge Hill engine at this time and the Lizzies were familiar on the best Liverpool services from their building right through to withdrawal. By this time the engine was in red livery with LMS style lining (46207 was similar). Photograph Alec Swain, B.P. Hoper Collection.

46200 on Nielston bank near Barrhead, on the Glasgow-Kilmarnock line; the time would be the last year of the locomotive's working life, 1962, for it carries a Kingmoor 12A plate. THE PRINCESS ROYAL was transferred there for the first time in April 1962 and was withdrawn at the end of that year. Photograph J. Robertson, B.P. Hoper Collection.

An unlikely location for a Lizzie, Stirling shed in the early 1960s – note speedo cable and AWS reservoir; these were fitted in November 1957 and July 1959 respectively. 46200 would presumably have worked the Anglo-Scottish car carrier. Photograph Derek A. Potton, B.P. Hoper Collection.

Scurrying through the landscape at Forteviot, south of Perth, 11 June 1962. The train looks like fish wagons, ex-Aberdeen perhaps, with 46200 having taken over at Perth. Readers might recall from the text the ignominy of 6200 failing with a hot box ('the hot box overheated'!) on its publicity run in August 1933. It turns out to have been an altogether more exciting affair if the story quoted by Rowledge is correct – the dauntless driver clambered out through the front window (they were hinged for cleaning) and doused the offending axle with oil, which promptly burst in to flame! He really should have got a medal. Photograph B.P. Hoper Collection.

strictions, the whistle was fitted in horizontally.

The front bogie had side bolsters and a carefully worked-out arrangement of lateral control springs. It was long for a bogie; 7ft. 6in., and bar frames were employed to reduce the weight so far as possible. It was to all intents a Churchward-De Glehn bogie; the basic principle was that, unlike other bogies, the weight transfer was separate from the pivot point, and lateral control.

Weight was transferred by the side bearers, while lateral control was by means of the helical coil springs around the pivot point. It had the effect of taking the loco, or part of it, from the means of lateral control, and thereby improving the ability of the bogie to 'control' the 'movement' of the locomotive on curves. Hence the 'ride' was greatly improved.

Great attention was given to the riding quality overall, in which the leading bogie played so vital a part; *The Rail-*

way Gazette described it thus: '*Special attention has been given to the bearing springs of the coupled wheels, and this, in conjunction with a bolster-type bogie and truck, is calculated to ensure a smooth running locomotive. A ribbed section of steel plate is used for the springs, the material being silico-manganese steel, whilst the plates are fixed in the buckle by means of a wedge cotter. The spring hangers are of the screwed type with knuckle thread, so that independent ad-*

Even under the shadow of modernisation, that extraordinary barrel length is still impressive indeed – 46200 leaves Crewe with the 9.20am to Holyhead, 28 July 1961. Photograph Alec Swain, B.P. Hoper Collection.

46201 PRINCESS ELIZABETH

Built Crewe
LM 'date built' 3 November 1933
Renumbered 6201 to 46201 week ending 7/8/48

REPAIRS

All Crewe unless stated otherwise
Figure in brackets = weekdays out of traffic

16/3/34-29/3/34**LO**	27/6/46-7/8/46**HO** (36)
1/5/34-15/5/34**LO**	17/9/46-5/12/46**HO** (69)
24/7/34-2/8/34**LS**	14/6/47-15/8/47**HS** (54)
11/12/34-21/12/34**LO**	4/10/47-22/10/47**LO** (16)
12/3/35-28/3/35**LO**	10/2/48-8/3/48**LO** (24)
10/10/35-3/12/35**HG**	26/6/48-3/8/48**LO** (33)
10/1/36-31/1/36**HO** (19)	23/10/48-16/12/48**HG** (47)
13/4/36-23/4/36**LO** (10)	17/6/49-10/8/49**LC** (47)
24/10/36-7/11/36**HS** (13)	15/11/49-14/12/49**LC** (26)
4/9/37-29/10/37**HG** (48)	13/2/50-16/3/50**HI** (27)
10/7/38-15/8/38**LS** (31)	3/8/50-8/9/50**LC** (31)
13/5/39-29/5/39**HS** (14)	6/11/50-20/12/50**HC** (38)
21/8/39-2/9/39**LO** (12)	2/12/50-20/1/51**NC(Rect)** (21)
7/2/40-19/3/40**HG** (36)	25/4/51-28/5/51**LI** (28)
7/5/40-11/5/40**LO** (5)	26/7/51-29/8/51**LC(EO)** (29)
20/9/40-12/10/40**HO** (20)	15/12/51-26/4/52**HG** (111)
4/6/41-25/6/41**LS** (19)	6/2/53-10/3/53**LC(EO)** (27)
26/2/42-30/4/42**LS** (55)	16/10/53-17/11/53**LC(EO)** (27)
5/9/42-3/10/42**HG** (25)	16/7/54-17/9/54**HG** (54)
4/2/43-18/3/43**LO** (37)	27/9/54-1/10/54**NC(Rect)EO** (4)
28/10/43-31/12/43**HS** (55)	28/3/56-19/5/56**HG** (44)
21/4/44-27/4/44**LO** (6)	5/6/56-8/6/56**NC(Rect)EO** (3)
13/6/44-28/7/44**HO** (40)	18/7/56-3/8/56**LC(EO)** (7)
28/12/44-8/2/45**LS** (37)	1/1/57-2/2/57**HC(EO)** (28)
31/10/45-8/12/45**HG** (34)	6/5/57-11/6/57**LC** (31)
14/12/45-1/1/46**LO** (15)	2/10/57-5/10/57**NC(EO)** (3)
	19/11/57-11/1/58**LI** (44)
	6/10/58-23/12/58**HI** (67)
	- 1/1/59 **NC(Rect)** (2)
	17/4/59-14/5/59**LC** (23)
	18/2/60-4/6/60**HG** (91)

SHEDS

Camden 4/11/33
Polmadie 6/1/34
Camden 24/8/39
Longsight 15/7/39
Camden 16/9/39
Edge Hill 21/10/39
Crewe North 5/10/40
Edge Hill 20/5/44
Crewe North 24/3/45
Edge Hill 11/12/48
Crewe North 13/6/53
'Scottish Region' 5/7/58
(later carried Polmadie
plate – 66A – by early 1959)
Carlisle Kingmoor 11/3/61
Carlisle Upperby 27/1/62

TENDERS

No	Fitted
9001	3/11/33
9066	28/3/35
9065	20/6/36
9373	28/11/36

MILEAGES

1933	7,191
1934	66,534
1935	51,084
1936	83,320
1937	77,789
1938	78,704
1939	65,156
1940	59,062
1941	61,301
1942	42,229
1943	30,340
1944	52,863
1945	49,823
1946	40,846
1947	52,846
1948	35,007
1949	54,309
1950	47,437
1951	50,733
1952	44,562
1953	47,364
1954	47,094
1955	74,485
1956	62,201
1957	53,425
1958	59,000 *'estimate'*
1959	58,203
1960	48,241
1961	2,569
1962	23,089

Mileage at 31/12/50 955,841
Mileage at 10/62 1,147,323
Withdrawn week ending 20/10/62
Preserved: *'Sold to Mr Bell (Elizabethan Society) 13th February 1963'*

---

justment can be obtained. As an experiment, one of these engines will be provided with compensating beams to enable observations to be made in order to ascertain whether a better running engine is thus obtained.' (This latter experiment, it seems, was never carried out.)

Most contemporary accounts remark approvingly of the commodious cab provided for the first Pacific, which had an excellent look-out for an engine of such bulk. The regulator was a pull-up one, 'conveniently placed and manipulated'. There was a Davies & Metcalfe exhaust-steam injector on the fireman's side and a Gresham & Craven live-steam injector on the driver's (left-hand) side. The standard LMS fittings were used where possible and all steam supplies to the various fittings controlled from the cab were taken from a manifold at the top of the firebox. It was vital to get enough 'primary air' straight on to the large grate and there were three separate damper doors, fitted at the front, middle and rear of the ashpan, with a separate control handle in the cab for each damper. Side dampers were also fitted, between the foundation ring and the ashpan, in order to give a good air supply at the sides of

The other one of the first pair – 6201, carrying a Camden 1B plate and a beautiful sight late in LMS days, at Polmadie. The vast new fireboxes of the Pacifics were a trial at first for many firemen, but it was found that the sloping grate could aid the work; coal could be piled under the door and the slope carried the coal forward. Photograph W. Hermiston, B.P. Hoper Collection.

That endless boiler barrel again, at Perth. The livery is green which all the Lizzies got from 1951-53 (some got red in 1958, but not PRINCESS ELIZABETH) and the tender bears the second emblem, introduced from 1957. The engine does not have AWS and, indeed, the Record Card does not mention any such fitting for 46201 – this engine and 46210 for some reason to do with their Scottish haunts never got the AWS. However, the speedo was fitted in October 1957, so the photograph definitely dates from after that time.

the grate. These side dampers were also controlled from the cab by means of a separate handle.

'The Hot Box Overheated'

6200 was shown off officially at Euston station on Wednesday 28 June 1933, in grey and without a name; it was the 'new Pacific type' without a hint as yet of the 'Princess Royal' name for engine and class. It would have been finished sooner, it would seem, for Bulleid describes Stanier going along to give his final blessing before the locomotive's unveiling. This was definitely not forthcoming, and it must have been a dismal scene as he drew increasingly annoyed attention to crude castings, patches of rust and so on. Mighty Crewe must have fallen silent when he compared the work unfavourably to – Swindon. It was another two weeks before the engine, now perfect, made its way to Euston for the show on 28 June. According to H.A.V. Bulleid, Stanier by this time had nicknamed it 'the Baby Austin'.

The great press trip took place on Tuesday 15 August 1933, with 6200 named by this time THE PRINCESS ROYAL. The train was made up of fourteen coaches including spare sleepers and a dynamometer car – an enormous total of 505 tons, the maximum permitted on the LMS at that time. It was scheduled non-stop Euston to Crewe on a 'Special Limit' time of 165 minutes, the same as that used for The Comet. 6200 started well, storming out of Euston with-

out a banker, which normally would have been served up for a train of this weight, and all 'without a vestige of slipping'. Progress was impressively regal, passing Willesden in under nine minutes, which was 'probably without precedent for a load of this magnitude'.

Most unfortunately, the parade was to be rained on, for shortly after passing Lichfield THE PRINCESS ROYAL developed a hot axle box, and the train had to be brought to a halt at 'Elmhurst siding', or Elmhurst Crossing as it seems to have been more properly known. It is probably the only time this name appears in the annals of British express steam locomotive development. After examination the train was allowed to proceed gingerly to Crewe. On the way, on the slow road, it suffered the humiliation of being overtaken by The Comet.

At Crewe the party was taken for a brief tour round the Works, to see the second and third Pacifics under construction. To make up for the embarrassment, a fast run was hastily set up for the return to London; a Royal Scot 6151

Right. The fateful log of 6200's press run of Tuesday 15 August 1933. The timing ends when the 'hot box overheated' south of Elmhurst Siding, after which the locomotive limped forward to Crewe. 6151 rattled the much reduced train back to London in good time. Cecil J. Allen (*British Pacific Locomotives*, Ian Allan, 1962) was on the train, and he recorded a speed of 86mph through King's Langley.

Engine : 4-cyl. 4-6-2, No. 6200.
Load : 14 coaches ; 500 tons tare, 505 tons gross.
Driver : Parsons (Crewe).

Distance.		Schedule.	Actual Times.	Max. and Min. Speeds.†
miles.		min.	m. s.	m.p.h.
0·0	EUSTON .. dep.	0	0 00	—
1·0	*Mile-post* pass		3 08	—
5·4	WILLESDEN JUNCTION ,,	9	8 47	61½
11·4	Harrow ,,		14 53	54
17·4	WATFORD JC. ,,	22	21 16	61½
24·5	Hemel Hempstead,,		28 31	54
31·7	TRING ,,	38	37 12	47½
40·2	Leighton ,,		44 50	75
46·7	BLETCHLEY ,,	51	50 13	—
52·4	Wolverton ,,		55 12	—
59·9	Roade ,,	63	62 22	54
62·8	Blisworth .. ,,	66	65 20	—
69·7	Weedon ,,		71 28	—
73·3	Welton ,,		76 40	—
82·6	RUGBY* ,,	86	84 11	40
91·4	Shilton ,,		94 28	—
97·1	NUNEATON ,,	101	99 56	69
106·5	Polesworth* ,,		108 42	40
110·0	TAMWORTH ,,	114	113 01	—
116·3	Lichfield ,,	120	119 30	—
118·8	Elmhurst Siding arr.		122 42	—

* Service slack. † At or near stations indicated.

Engine : 3-cyl. 4-6-0, No. 6151.
Load : 7 coaches ; 211 tons tare, 215 tons gross.
Driver : Parsons (Crewe).

Distance.		Actual Times.	Max. and Min. Speeds.†
miles.		m. s.	m.p.h.
0·0	CREWE .. .. dep.	0 00	—
		sigs.	
10·5	Whitmore .. pass	14 23	—
		sigs.	
19·2	Norton Bridge ,,	22 59	40
24·5	STAFFORD* .. ,,	27 57	40
33·8	Rugeley .. ,,	37 13	72½
41·8	Lichfield .. ,,	44 05	—
48·1	TAMWORTH .. ,,	49 06	77½
		p.w.s.	
55·8	Atherstone .. ,,	56 43	65
61·0	NUNEATON ... ,,	61 14	71½
66·1	*Mile-post 92* ,,	65 42	{67 / 77½}
75·5	RUGBY* .. ,,	73 32	42
82·8	Welton .. ,,	81 05	64
88·4	Weedon .. ,,	85 26	79
95·3	Roade .. ,,	99 11	67
103·7	Wolverton .. ,,	99 00	79½
111·4	BLETCHLEY .. ,,	103 50	—
117·9	Leighton .. ,,	109 14	—
122·0	Cheddington .. ,,	112 40	—
126·4	TRING .. ,,	116 38	67½
133·6	Hemel Hempstead.. ,,	122 16	85
140·7	WATFORD .. ,,	127 19	72½
146·7	Harrow .. ,,	132 12	80
152·7	WILLESDEN .. ,,	136 50	—
157·1	*Mile-post 1* ,,	141 20	—
157·6	*Mile-post ½* { arr.	142 30	—
	{ dep.	144 22	
158·1	EUSTON .. arr.	147 18	—

* Service slack. † At or near stations indicated.

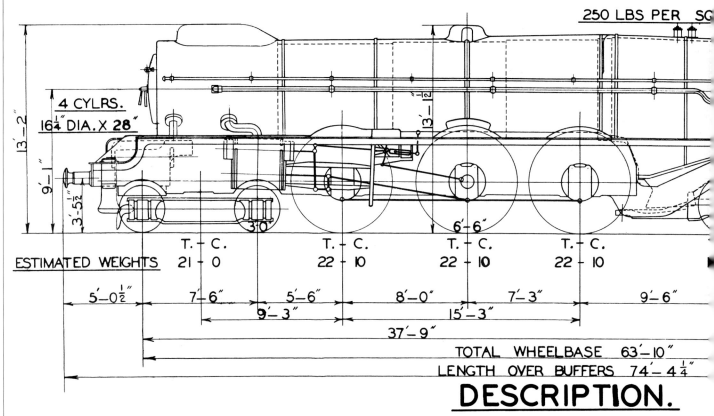

250 LBS PER SQ

4 CYLRS.
16¼" DIA. X 28"

13'-2"

9'-1"

3'-5½"

3|0

6'-6"

13'-12"

ESTIMATED WEIGHTS

	T. – C.	T. – C.	T. – C.	T. – C.
	21 – 0	22 – 10	22 – 10	22 – 10

5'-0½"   7'-6"   5'-6"   8'-0"   7'-3"   9'-6"

9'-3"   15'-3"

37'-9"

TOTAL WHEELBASE 63'-10"
LENGTH OVER BUFFERS 74'-4¼"

DESCRIPTION.

BOILER.   BARREL 20'-4" DIA. OUTS. 5'-9", INCREAS
FIREBOX.   OUTS. 8'-6" X 7'-1" & 6'-1". INS. 7'-7¾" X 6'-1" &

TUBES.
{
SUPERHEATER ELEMENTS 16.1⅜" DIA. OUTS
LARGE TUBES 16.5⅛" DIA. OUTS. X 7 S.W
SMALL TUBES 170. 2¼" DIA. OUTS. X 11 S.W
}

HEATING SURFACE.
{
TUBES   2523·0 SQ.FT.
FIREBOX   190·0   "   "
SUPERHEATER 370·0   "   "
} TOTAL 2

GRATE AREA.   45·0   "   "
TRACTIVE EFFORT AT 85% B.P. 40,300 LBS.

4 – 6 – 2 PASSENGE

ROYAL HORSE GUARDSMAN was rustled up and the 'makeweight' coaches taken off to leave just seven vehicles, weighing 215 tons. Driver Albert Parsons and Fireman Harry Betley, both of Crewe North, worked both trains and, in the opinion of *The Railway Gazette*, '*deserved the congratulations offered to them on arrival at Euston, for the excellent handling of the two locomotives concerned.*' It was the leading coupled axlebox which ran hot, but (some things never change) the press did not get it quite right. *The Daily Mail* gave a splendid description of 6200 storming the 'one in *seven*' (!) out of Euston, while a report in another (unnamed) newspaper gave *The Railway Gazette* some fine fun. According to the anonymous reporter 'the hot box over-

heated'. '*Are we to understand*' thundered the *RG*, '*that every locomotive carries a hot box about with it as a matter of course and this is liable at any time to become overheated? On that assumption may not the superheater itself become super-super-heated or the safety valves, having forsaken their function, allow the boiler to boil over? These are terrifying thoughts indeed and we hope they may never be translated into anything more serious than the picturesque and even romantic language sometimes employed by reporters in the columns of certain daily newspapers. The hot box, by common consent, is a confounded nuisance and there is nothing to be gained by subjecting it to the process of making confusion worse confounded*'

Steaming
Stanier used a sixteen element superheater in 6200, following practice established at Swindon. This, it was soon realised, was a mistake; this size was inadequate and 32 elements became the standard – the convoluted details are given in the various 'Phase' tables. The strange thing was that, to the railway press of the time, the lack of a sufficient level of superheating seemed only too apparent, right from the start. *The Railway Gazette* devoted editorial space to the perceived shortcomings, and this must have seemed an appallingly public scrutiny of his work to Stanier, still out to prove himself on the LMS. Worse, *The Railway Engineer* (don't forget, these were not breathless enthusiast maga-

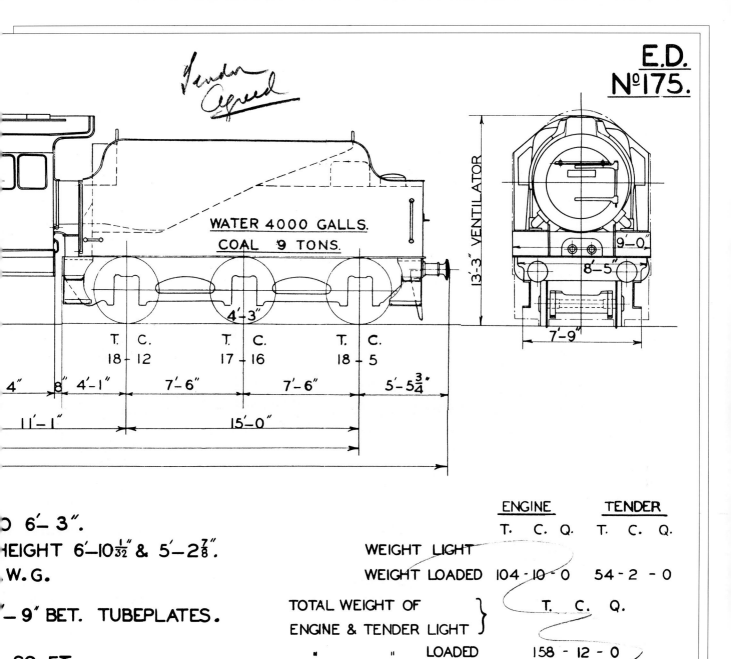

Tender Agreed

WATER 4000 GALLS.
COAL 9 TONS.

13'-3" VENTILATOR

9'-0"

8'-5"

7'-9"

4'-3"

T.	C.		T.	C.		T.	C.
18	12		17	16		18	5

4"   8"   4'-1"   7'-6"   7'-6"   5'-5¾"

11'-1"   15'-0"

○ 6'-3".

HEIGHT 6'-10¹⁄₃₂" & 5'-2⁷⁄₈".

W.G.

─ 9' BET. TUBEPLATES.

SQ. FT.

NGINE.

	ENGINE			TENDER		
	T.	C.	Q.	T.	C.	Q.
WEIGHT LIGHT						
WEIGHT LOADED	104	10	0	54	2	0
TOTAL WEIGHT OF ENGINE & TENDER LIGHT }				T.	C.	Q.
" " LOADED				158	12	0

L. M. & S. R.

LOCOMOTIVE DRAWING OFFICE,
DERBY.

---

zines but the respected trade journals of railways world-wide) joined in: '*It may be said that an express locomotive working for a large percentage of its time with steam at a high rate of expansion requires more superheat than a goods engine where the steam is not used at such a high expansion rate. It is questionable whether full consideration has been given to this point...*'

Alarmingly, even the readers joined in, and though Mr John Poole, M.I.Loco.E. was probably over – or rather under – stating it when he declared that '*the new engines will not better the performance of the Royal Scot class*' he was spot-on when he declared '*they would have been infinitely better if fitted with a 36in. combustion chamber and at least 32*

elements'. Thirty-two elements it duly was for the class, and the early steaming difficulties disappeared. Matters were actually rather more complicated than this – again, see the various 'Phases' tabulated later in the book.

It is not clear if this very public (for those times at least) examination of the new loco's possible deficiencies have any parallel. It was typical of the time that it was muted and respectful; *The Railway Engineer* for instance, could not go further out of its way to praise the new locomotive (*The Railway Gazette* was the same in this regard). Take this last comment, almost Victorian in its careful structure: '*The new engine is a remarkably fine production, and by its performance it may be expected to justify fully its*

Above. Outline diagram of a Princess Royal, dated 28 March 1934. This shows the 'short' firebox of the first two, not the 'long' firebox that was to appear on the 1935 batch of ten and indeed this is an original drawing, amended to show a) a rather funny streamlined cowl round the chimney (a manifestation of the streamlining debate then underway) and b) the proposed new tender. On the original a new piece of paper has simply been glued over the old straight sided tender and the new drawing made over it. *Tender Agreed* is written in pencil – this is of course, the second 'standard' tender, fitted for a while until the new ten ton high sided ones were built. The weights would change of course, for those shown relate to 6200 as built - they have been scribbled through in pencil.

introduction and prove a decided asset to the railway company in the conduct of its long distance express passenger traffic.'

'High Speed Possibilities'

Before 6200 suffered its hot box, it had covered 5,000 miles on running-in and trial work, without any hint of trouble in this regard. No definite explanation could be found, apart from ill-fortune. No conclusions could really be drawn from the failure, and there was no reason to expect this to be a weakness in the design. Though it somewhat took the shine off the Big Day, the fact remained that the new Pacific had put in a remarkable performance, ascending Camden's 1 in 77 and 105 without assistance or trace of a slip. Plainly, the existing LMS main line schedules contained much room for improvement. The time was coming, it was clear, when the Pacifics would play their proper part in faster West Coast trains.

The second LMS Pacific, 6201 PRINCESS ELIZABETH, was not ready until November 1933, so for some months 6200 was the only one running on the LMS, closely observed to determine its capabilities on a variety of express work.

Without, so far as can be determined, a hint of hot box trouble, THE PRINCESS ROYAL carried on impressing both its owners and observers. It turned in a run of some considerable note on the evening of Friday 6 April 1933. The 5.25pm express out of Liverpool Lime Street to Euston had the fastest booking on the LMS, covering the 152.7 miles Crewe to Willesden Junction in 142 minutes. The new Pacific, it was clear, could eat even this schedule, for with twelve coaches weighing 380 tons fully laden it covered the distance in less than 135 minutes, at an average speed of 68mph, despite several signal checks which cost nearly three minutes. This, it was announced, was the 'quickest time which has yet been made from Crewe to Willesden'. The dynamic Driver A. Parsons of Crewe North was once again in charge. *(See below left).*

By the autumn of 1933 THE PRINCESS ROYAL was pounding the length of the West Coast, though it was working London to Carlisle rather than to Glasgow. Size limitations in the firebox, as we have seen, meant that Carlisle was the effective limit of efficient running for Royal Scots. They could get to the border, it seems, but progress beyond would be hopelessly compromised by a be-clinkered grate, though ashpan capacity was perhaps the real issue. This was long before rocking grates, which would not appear on Royal Scots for many years, and even then, a lot of drivers were very chary of using them on the road. It only took one disaster of a fire lost or the grate not moving back into position to make a bloke extremely reluctant to try it again, whatever the 'guvnors might say.

Yet it seems at first to have been more convenient, in operating terms, to work the new Pacific to Carlisle and back rather than into Scotland. After its Liverpool exploits, it was put on longer runs – the daily pounding up and down the line rather than headline catching forays. Later in the year it was making a double trip to Carlisle, 299 miles each way, throughout the week. The engine worked up non-stop on the Royal Scot, arriving at Euston at 5.45pm, returning to Carlisle with the 11pm night train out of the capital. A long association with night

L.M.S.R. CREWE-EUSTON. Engine : 4-6-2 No. 6200, *The Princess Royal.* Load 12 = 354 tons tare, 380 tons full. Driver : A. Parsons (Crewe).				
Distance.		Schedule.	Actual.	Speeds
miles.		min.	min.sec.	m.p.h.
0·0	CREWE	0	0 00	—
4·8	Betley Road	—	6 45	59
10·5	Whitmore	—	12 26	58½*
14·7	Standon Bridge	—	15 46	77½
19·2	Norton Bridge	—	19 11	82†
24·5	STAFFORD††	26	23 11	38¶
28·6	Milford	—	27 36	67
33·8	RUGELEY	36	31 55	78
37·1	Armitage	—	34 29	75
41·8	LICHFIELD	42	38 13	—
48·1	TAMWORTH	—	42 45	85§
51·6	Polesworth	—	45 36	68§
55·8	Atherstone	—	49 13	65
61·0	NUNEATON	60	53 35	76½
64·6	Bulkington	—	56 38	70¾
70·0	Bunklow	—	60 53	80½
74·9	*Rugby No. 7*	—	sigs.	15½
75·5	RUGBY††	73	66 44	—
77·8	Hillmorton	—	70 03	57¼
82·8	Welton	—	75 15	76½
88·4	Weedon	—	79 48	72¶
95·3	BLISWORTH	—	85 26	74
98·2	ROADE	94	87 57	68½
103·3	Castlethorpe	—	91 49	85
105·7	Wolverton	—	93 40	72
111·4	BLETCHLEY	105	98 24	75
			sigs.	
117·9	Leighton	—	103 51	64¶
122·0	Cheddington	—	107 39	61¼
126·4	TRING	119	112 09	55¼
130·1	Berkhamsted	—	115 38	72½
137·2	King's Langley	—	120 58	83¼
140·7	WATFORD	—	123 33	79*
144·8	Hatch End	—	126 52	71½
146·7	Harrow	—	128 25	74
150·0	Wembley	—	131 09	—
			sigs.	30¶
152·7	WILLESDEN JC.	142	134 37	—

* Minimum Madeley Bank (1 m. 177).
† Maximum, Great Bridgeford.
¶ Speed reduced by brakes.
†† Service slack.
§ Maximum, Hademore trough.
‡ Attained speed, Kilsby Tunnel.

46201 at some speed, passing Wandlemill (on the southbound climb to Beattock) with an up train, 16 July 1960. While 6200 did many tests, 6201 also ran its share, most famously from Euston to Glasgow and back on 16-17 November 1936 – described by various authors as the highlight of the Princess Royals' careers. The test was to pave the way for the new Coronation Scot, planned for the following year. 6201 had a speedometer specially fitted for the occasion, which recorded extended periods at more than 80mph, with peaks of over 90. The surprise was that the resulting Coronation Scot was not timed more boldly. Photograph J.L. Stevenson.

work was thus established early on for the Pacifics. Once the second Pacific became available later on in the year, it was intended that the 4-6-2s would work through to Glasgow, 401½ miles, though this would mean a lower *daily* mileage for each.

In fact, the whole reasoning behind equipping the LMS, however fitfully, with a fleet of Pacifics was – if we go back to the original publicity for 6200 – for a service of 500 ton trains between London and Glasgow, unaided over both Shap and Beattock. It was quite a 'spec.' by any measure, and there would only be a stop for crew changing, either at Crewe or Carlisle. The Second World War and the general declining trend in coal quality and available labour from the 1930s made many holes in this grand plan but many of the through working components of Stanier's 1932 'Pacific Plan' – with the Coronations rather more than the Princesses of course – was there to see more or less through to the take-over by the EE Type 4 diesels in the early 1960s.

Yet it was the end of 1935 before even a dozen Pacifics were available and for two years only the first pair, together with the turbo one, were running. This was not going to bring about a revolution in Anglo-Scottish services and the Princesses seemed to spend more time on spectacular trials and tests in 1934-35 than in bringing about any particular revolution in the day to day running – though of course their 'day in day out' work was on ordinary service trains. There was a further high speed test for instance on Thursday 27 June 1935, when there were still only two conventional Pacifics running – though in a matter of days the rest of the Princesses would begin entering traffic. 6200 THE PRINCESS ROYAL made a test run with the 5.25pm Liverpool Lime Street to Euston once more; it was still the fastest start to stop booking on the LMS, 142 minutes for the 152.7 miles Crewe to Willesden Junction (hence its repeated choice for the test) and the average speed was 64.5mph. The usual load was 300-360 tons but for 6200 the train was increased to fifteen vehicles including dynamometer car – 475 tons fully loaded. 6200 fair ran away with this, arriving at Euston no less than fourteen minutes early on a schedule of three hours and

Forteviot, on the line to Perth and 46201, near the end of its life, hurries along with a mix of empty carriage stock and vans, with a milk tank at the rear. Withdrawn near the end of October 1962, the engine was 'sold to Mr Bell (Elizabethan Society)' according to the Record Card, and was dumped out of use at Kingmoor. On 12 August 1963 it left there under its own steam, *The Railway Observer* reported, travelling via Settle, Leeds Sheffield and Derby to Saltley, where it arrived two days later. From there it went to its new home at Ashchurch for display but tunnel clearances on the way meant that part of the motion had to be dismantled and it was towed dead down the Lickey by 4F 44045. Photograph N. Swift, B.P. Hoper Collection.

twenty minutes for the 193.7 miles from Liverpool to London with two stops, Crewe and Willesden. Between the last two points the Princess had averaged over seventy miles an hour.

The Princess Royal Pacifics were, in a curious way, a sort of 'false start' for the LMS. They took a long time to appear in any kind of numbers and even at their maximum numbers were hardly enough to run a reconstituted, upgraded West Coast service. Oddly, as the LMS gained experience with its Pacifics, it became clear that something rather different was required. The Princesses did indeed 'transmute' into the Coronation Pacifics; the order in the 1937 Building Programme started out as an order for more Princesses, which simply emerged at the other end as the wholly and radically different first five Coronations, 6220-6224. With that, Princess Royal

building was over. Commercial events had overtaken the Princess engines and the anticipated West Coast speed improvements looked to be overshadowed by streamlined and highly publicity-friendly events on the East Coast. The Coronations, if you like, were 'Improved Princesses', and the engines' 'high water mark' was effectively the two runs of 16-17 November 1936. The new Coronation Scot would go into service the following year come what may, and 6201 did a return trip London to Glasgow, to investigate the performance possibilities available in an engine of this sort. It was fairly climactic stuff, Cecil J. Allen writing that it was 'with little doubt the most notable round trip ever undertaken by an engine of the original Princess Royal series'.

An extra man was provided on the footplate in the event of problems, for the

runs were non-stop in both directions – all three were Crewe North men of course, for these were the only crews that knew the entire route Glasgow-London. 6201 PRINCESS ELIZABETH (now with a 32 element superheater) took a seven coach test train (with dynamometer car) both ways London to Glasgow; both runs were remarkable, with the time cut to just under 5¾ hours coming back south on the second day. This involved an average speed the whole way in excess of 70 mph. It was odd that this special effort served only to confirm that the Princesses, in a year, would become the 'B Team' in the LMS Pacific fleet!

Change Afoot

It is useful to divide the Princess Pacifics into three – the first two which provided a proving ground for subsequent engines, the Turbomotive which by any conceiv-

able measure stands entirely alone, and the subsequent ten engines 6203-6212, which it is tempting to call the 'production series'.

Before the 1935 batch appeared, a number of small changes had been made to the first two Pacifics. 6201 got a particularly horrible stovepipe double chimney in October 1934 but this was soon removed when the particular double blastpipe arrangement employed proved not to work well at all. Rowledge (*The LMS Pacifics*, David & Charles, 1987) describes it as unusual in British practice, for the inside cylinders discharged separately from the outside ones, the former through the front blastpipe nozzle, the latter through the rear nozzle. (SR Lord Nelson 4-6-0 865, incidentally, had a similar arrangement in 1938.) 6201 was rapidly altered back to a single blastpipe with normal chimney. Oval buffers appeared instead of the

round ones but it was the steaming deficiencies, and the boiler alterations consequent upon solving them, that brought about a sequence of detail changes.

The disappointing steaming emanated from the shortcomings of the superheater (as predicted by outside observers at the time) and proved bothersome at first. All manner of tinkering went on, but in the end only a wholly bigger superheater arrangement resolved matters. From hereon, the boiler changes within this small class tended to dictate external appearance, and they are dealt with later under the heading *A Complication of Boilers* – 'complication', in this instance, being a perfect collective noun. Tenders changed too; these were not nearly so fiendish in their complexity and are also dealt with separately.

Two views of 46201 at Glasgow Central Platform 3 on 28 March 1959; in the first it backs down past fellow Polmadie resident 46222 QUEEN MARY on the Royal Scot. After the 'Big Lizzie' leaves, PRINCESS ELIZABETH makes her own way out, with 'the Birmingham' in fine style. Photographs J. Robertson, B.P. Hoper Collection.

The front end of 6202, the bulbous casings giving a rather more powerful look than was evident on the other two Princesses, 6200 and 6201.

TURBOMOTIVE

'An interesting development...' The Locomotive, 15 July 1935.

So, with the Executive Committee (see its deliberations, right) prepared to authorise the extra cost involved, 'the Turbomotive' – usually called simply 'the Turbo' – was born. In this sense it was very reminiscent of FURY a few years before. The extract above was the culmination of LMS interest in turbine developments that had begun the previous year, when the first Pacifics were planned. Stanier 'nipped over to Sweden' (in the words of H.A.V. Bulleid) to inspect a non-condensing turbine locomotive built as a result of collaboration between Metropolitan Vickers and the Swedish Ljungström firm. The trip seems to have gone well, and Stanier elected to 'have a try', as the memorandum at the head of this section records.

This new sort of turbine operation offered advantages over the older condensing 'turbo' locos – less weight, less awkward mechanical parts to go expensively wrong and less hammer blow, all making for altogether smoother running. The arguments were similar in a way to those for four cylinders on the conven-

Top. Official LMS portrait of 6202; it was immediately dubbed 'the Turbomotive', for obvious reasons. On the right-hand side, this was the reverse turbine, which gave rather more trouble than the other, main, turbine, which lay between the frames. The basic problem, however, was of imperfect turbine lubrication. Oil whirled around inside the turbines, forced at pressure by various pumps; there was even a steam driven reciprocating pump which kept working for half an hour after the locomotive came to a halt, so that the bearings were played with oil and cooled slowly.

LONDON MIDLAND AND SCOTTISH RAILWAY COMPANY.

MECHANICAL & ELECTRICAL
ENGINEERING COMMITTEE.

Euston Station.

22nd February, 1933.

Provision of Turbine Gear Driven Locomotive.

Submitted memorandum (14th February 1933) from the Chief Mechanical Engineer and the Chief Operating Manager, together with covering memorandum from the Vice Presidents (Sir Harold Hartley and Mr. Lemon) recommending that one of the three four-cylinder 4-6-2 class locomotives, authorised by Mechanical & Electrical Engineering Committee Minute No.142 and Traffic Committee Minute No.3221 of the 27th July, 1932, be built as a geared turbine locomotive, in order that comparative trials may be made between this type of driving mechanism and the ordinary reciprocating gear.

Turbine locomotives with condensers had been tried on the L.M.S. system on two previous occasions but had proved unreliable in service, but the locomotive it was proposed to construct would have a non-condensing turbine, developed by the Ljungstrom Company, the arrangement consisting of a main turbine driving the coupled wheels through totally enclosed gears running in oil, and the exhaust led up the chimney, an outline of the locomotive being shewn on diagram E.U.149 submitted.

Messrs. Metropolitan-Vickers who have taken up the rights of manufacture in this country of the Ljungstrom turbine drive for locomotives were satisfied as to its commercial possibilities and were prepared to supply the turbine and gearing, including quill drive, for £6,000.

The estimated cost of the new standard 4-6-2 engine without tender was £8,075, and the cost of the same engine fitted with a turbine and gearing, after making allowance for not having to provide cylinders, motion and other standard parts, would be approximately £13,500.

The submission of the proposal had the approval of the Executive Committee, who were of the opinion that it was desirable to investigate this new type of locomotive even if it did not hold out immediate possibilities of financial savings, and whilst the increased cost of interest would be £270 per annum, it was anticipated there would be a saving of at least £150 per annum in coal consumption, with additional improvement in performance.

The Chairman stated that the proposal had been recommended to the Board by the Traffic Committee, subject to reference to the Mechanical & Electrical Engineering Committee

Approved.

Left-hand side of the new locomotive. The bulbous casing over the bogie did not contain the forward turbine, as is often said, for this lay between the frames; under the case was the control equipment, pumps, oil sump and so on. The control rods and suchlike ran along the left-hand side, under the full casing.

tional Pacifics. Minor increases in coal or water consumption were not thought important; the big disadvantage was higher capital cost.

The turbine loco had to be operationally comparable to the other two Pacifics – that is, capable of 500 tons London to Glasgow and it was decided that the turbine should be 2,000hp, using steam at 250lb with a steam tempera-

ture of something like 750°F. 2,000hp is the figure quoted in the contemporary press; 2,600 is the figure in subsequent common currency – this figure apparently represents the horsepower developed at 62mph.

The main motive power unit was a multi-stage turbine; it is frequently quoted as being carried on the left-hand side of the frame, but the turbine was

fairly and squarely placed centrally between the frames. It was the control equipment, oil pumps and so on that were on the left-hand side. This forward turbine had treble reduction, double helical gear, completely enclosed in a fabricated gear case suspended from three supports on the engine frame and restrained from moving sideways relative to the turbine. The turbine was permanently meshed

6202 'THE TURBOMOTIVE'

Built Crewe
LM 'date built' 29 June 1935
Renumbered 6202 to 46202 week ending 12/3/49
'Converted to reciprocating type at HG repair 15/8/52'
'Redesignated 'Princess Anne' type'

MILEAGES

1935	9,815
1936	73,268
1937	45,441
1938	44,176
1939	12,998
1940	-
1941	6,314
1942	33,702
1943	30,618
1944	3,521
1945	61,524
1946	12,358
1947	39,230
1948	23,101
1949	45,563
1950	17,143
1951	Nil
Conversion	
1952	11,443
1953	Nil
1954	Nil

'Total miles run as a turbine locomotive 458,772'
Mileage at 6/5/50 458,772
Withdrawn week ending 22/5/54
Ruined in Harrow & Wealdstone accident 8/10/52, 'date actually broken up' given as 22/5/54

TENDERS

No	Fitted
9003	29/6/35
9003	15/8/52

(eventually went to 8F 48134)

SHEDS

Camden 29/6/35
Edge Hill 22/2/36
Camden 19/4/36
Crewe North 16/9/39
Camden 9/8/41
Crewe North 27/6/53

This last 'move' to Crewe North was surely the most peculiar allocation in BR history, though the mortal remains of 46202 were not too far away, in the works. The place being kept warm in the complement (perhaps this was the reason) would soon be filled by DUKE OF GLOUCESTER.

REPAIRS
All Crewe unless stated otherwise
Figure in brackets
= weekdays out of traffic

24/9/35-21/12/35**LO** (77)
15/1/36-4/2/36**LO** (18)
15/5/36-24/6/36**LO** (35)
14/7/36-31/7/36**HO** (16)
28/1/37-13/4/37**LO** (64)
- 11/11/37**TRO** (22)
29/11/37-16/12/37**LO** (16)
2/6/38-24/10/38**LS** (124)
8/2/39-31/7/39**LO** (148)
17/7/41-14/7/42**LO** (257)
1/8/42-8/8/42**LO** (7)
21/11/42-9/1/43**LO** (42)
11/6/43-22/9/44**HG** (402)
18/12/44-18/1/45**LO** (27)
12/4/45-1/6/45**LO** (43)
12/7/45-25/7/45**LO** (12)
9/3/46-8/4/47**HG** (337)
16/8/47-9/9/47**NC** (21)
23/9/47-12/10/47**NC** (20)
5/12/47-3/1/48**LO** (25)
16/4/48-10/3/49**LC** (280)
13/6/49-22/6/49**LC** (9)
27/9/49-14/12/49**NC** (16)
21/12/49-17/1/50**LC** (22)
18/2/50-23/2/50**NC** (4)
17/3/50-13/4/50**NC** (22)
6/5/50-15/8/52**HG** (708)
(Conversion to conventional loco)

The Turbomotive at Lime Street about 1938. The first boiler was similar to those of the second batch of ten Princesses; in fact the first of the boilers intended for the ten, with 32 superheater element, was 'diverted' to the turbine project. The regulator was combined in the superheater header. Of two spare boilers built one, with 40 superheater elements, replaced the 'Turbo's' first boiler, in July 1936 – this had a dome to house the regulator. The Turbomotive was out of action for such protracted periods that this boiler, No.9236, could be used on other Princesses in the meantime!

with the leading coupled axle though there was flexibility in the final drive, to absorb the continuous shocks and bumps of life out on the road – predictably, it was here where many of the worst problems were to be encountered.

For reverse running, a separate turbine was provided, fitted on the right-hand side. There was an additional single reduction gear for it and for revers-

ing there was therefore: 'a quadruple reduction gear between the turbine spindle and the driving axle'. The method of operation necessarily differed radically from any orthodox locomotive, and provision had to be made for reversing by means of a dog clutch, situated between the reverse turbine and the final drive.

The forward turbine was permanently connected through to the trans-

mission gear and, therefore, when the reverse turbine was in operation, the steam supply to the forward turbine was cut off and the drive from the reverse turbine engaged by means of a steam operated arrangement. This could only be achieved when the Turbomotive was stationary, and a safety device was incorporated in the transmission to prevent the change being made while it was in motion. When

'The Turbo' stands at Euston; the radiator between the frames at the front was of course just one more of the peculiar and unexpected features of this machine. The oil being forced around the turbine system passed through this straightforward air-cooling radiator, much like the water in a car engine, and was protected by non-return valves. The flap was raised during running to force as much air as possible over the radiator. Drivers were instructed to ensure it was raised and a pair of oil gauges in the cab indicated oil temperatures before and after cooling. The radiator reduced the oil temperature from something like 140° to below 100°F. Photograph B.P. Hoper Collection.

The 'Turbo', in fine condition, waits to depart Euston early on in its career. Note the anxious body of white-aproned attendants, including, probably, the resident fitter (in flat cap); there was need of oil that day!

the drive from the reverse turbine was engaged, its steam supply could then be opened – from this, it follows that when the Turbomotive was running tender first, the forward turbine blades moved in the reverse direction.

The steam supply was simply kept fully 'on' while running, the regulator acting just as an 'on/off' valve while the engine was in motion. From this 'valve-regulator' steam went to regulators on the nozzles of the two turbines – six on the forward turbine and three on the reverse unit. These were operated from the 'control box' in the cab, and by means of suitable inter-locking devices between the reversing clutch mechanism and the turbine regulators, it was impossible to admit steam to the forward turbine when the reverse was in gear, or vice versa.

All the bearings for the turbines, transmission gears and so on were lubricated mechanically from a gear pump submerged in an oil well at the rear end of the gear casing.

In other respects the locomotive was a Princess Royal – the taper boiler worked at 250lb, the barrel plates and firebox wrapper plates were in 2% nickel steel to keep down the weight. The turbine propulsion did require a considerable modification to the layout of the smokebox, however; the low pressure exhaust which resulted from the turbine arrangement made a double blastpipe necessary. *The Locomotive* (though it reads as if 6202 had a conventional blast pipe – in fact it had a twin blastpipe) describes it thus: *'The orifice of the blast pipe is varied automatically by means of a central cone dart which is raised or lowered as the number of steam nozzles for the turbine in increased or decreased. Another unusual feature is the provision of a radiator at the front for oil cooling.'*

The whole design and performance of the Turbomotive was covered at great length and detail by Roland Bond, in a paper to the Institution of Locomotive Engineers, in 1946; Rowledge, drawing on this and much else besides, has made an excellent and most accessible account in *The LMS Pacifics*. There is also a very full account by John Horton in *Bedside Backtrack* (Atlantic, 1993). The complications and vicissitudes of the 'Turbo' were many and various and only an outline of the main points have been attempted here... It was an experimental machine and the fact that it spent

'Turbo', in works as ever. It carries a Camden shed plate, so the period would be 1936-1939. As to which particular works visit is involved, that would be anyone's guess! The loco's innards lie here and there. It is easy to over-emphasise its shortcomings with respect to mileage and availability. For an experimental engine it put up very creditable show; there can be no other 'experiment' that, when it was working, did so well... Photograph H.N. James.

The Turbomotive makes a fairly stately descent into Euston in the 1930s. A regular on the London-Liverpool run, it was at Edge Hill only briefly; for the rest of the time was a Camden engine. A principal job, incidentally, was the 5.25pm, long the fastest run on the LMS and the stage of those tests with 6200 in 1933 and 1935. With its unique problems it was of course highly desirable that the turbine loco should be stationed at one shed where staff could become familiar with its day-to-day eccentricities. This was only common sense, though doubtless the Camden blokes would have been happy to see it go somewhere else for some other mug to look after.

lengthy periods in works can hardly be regarded as startling – the only surprise, possibly, is that the LMS kept it going so long. Throughout the 1930s it suffered expensive failures out on the road, and unlike its conventional counterparts, there was rarely any hope of 'limping' home. It was mainly the reverse turbine that failed, and most problems had lubrication deficiencies at their heart. With delays in obtaining spare parts and the need sometimes to send items to Metrovick, delays grew – two spells out of service following failure of the forward turbine cost over two months out of traf-

fic in one instance and nearly *five* months in the other. With a fleet of the things, of course, this sort of delay would have been reduced markedly; the turbines might even have been good candidates for 'component replacement', though to hoist out a complete forward turbine would presumably have meant removing the boiler too. Whatever, with more of them in service, the problems deriving from lack of familiarity and expertise on the part of drivers and fitters would fade.

The turbine locomotive was set aside upon the outbreak of the Second World War, and that should have been

the end of it. The LMS did this with all the Coronations of course (see *The Book of the Coronation Pacifics*) until it was realised (very quickly) that such machines would be needed more than ever. The 'Turbo' stayed in store, for it was rightly realised that Metropolitan Vickers would not be able to give it their regular attention. This was true, but such were the exigencies of war that 6202 was eventually drawn out of store and put back to work, with no heed to the difficulties. The need was for locos, any locos, to work the traffic. The engine had only gone back into traffic in August 1939,

With radiator flap fully open, 'Turbo' shows its mettle; when working fully, it was marginally superior to the other Lizzies.

The 'turbo' waits to leave Euston in the 1930s. Generally it would work down with the 10.40am to Liverpool in the morning and back with the 5.25 teatime train, or it would leave London in the evening about 6 'o'clock, returning with the mid-morning train the next day. The engine had horsepower to spare over the other Princesses and was comparable on any duties except when it was 'playing up'. Test comparisons showed it to be more powerful than the others in some small measure and slightly more economical with fuel. Note the attendant fitter with empty oil can.

following its heroic five months overhaul but had promptly been stored, as mentioned above. It was dragged out of retirement in the Crewe Paint Shop in July 1941, in a spirit of hurling everything into the fray, but it is doubtful whether the continued works attention made this worthwhile. With Metropolitan Vickers all-out on war work, the delays following any fault were gargantuan – over a year in one case when it ruined much of its vitals merely moving around the shed yard. Over 1946-47 it spent nearly an-

other year 'on the blocks'. In the rather frostier economic climes of the late 1940s, with chronic shortages of labour and materials it was rightly considered that all the expense and effort involved in getting 6202 running again would not be worthwhile. It made more sense to rebuild it as a conventional Pacific, to join the admittedly thin ranks of the London Midland 7Ps. The 'Turbo' was officially withdrawn in March 1950 and in May the following year BR, surveying the collection of parts, authorised their rebuilding

into one Pacific. The result was 46202 PRINCESS ANNE, a curious hybrid of Princess Royal and Coronation 4-6-2. With its lower pitched boiler it was indubitably a Princess, though the big casing associated with the steam pipes and the Coronation cylinders gave it a distinctively Coronation look. It was, in effect, 'Lizzie meets Big Lizzie'. Some official details ordered include:
'Boiler in range 6203-6212 with regulator in dome
Inside cylinders – cast steel 'Coronation'

The Turbomotive in BR black at Edge Hill in July 1949, showing the extended casing fitted following modifications to the reverse turbine. No precise date seems to available for this modification, which would have followed one of the wartime failures. The engine was an elusive beast and the 'bush telegraph' was important in getting any view of it. To the lineside oiks it was always 'the Turbo' and its strange unchanging 'whoosh' of an exhaust was always somewhat startling. It was the weakness of this exhaust that led to the fitting of smoke deflectors. It rode well by all accounts but was considered dirty, so far as the footplate was concerned. The equable motion made it difficult to judge speed and a 'speed indicator' was fitted in 1943 – it was alone among the LMS Pacifics in retaining this equipment in the War. Photograph R.K. Blencowe Collection.

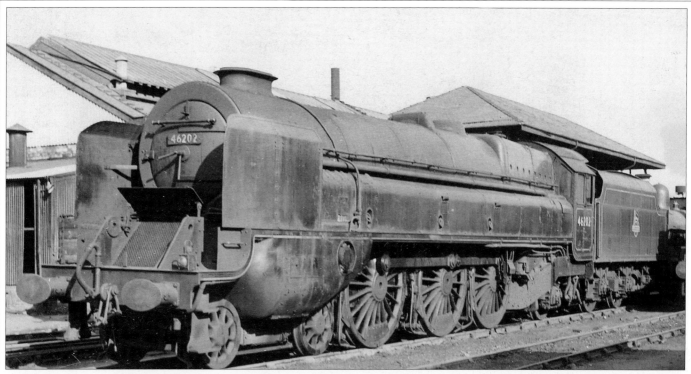

The Turbomotive in Crewe works Yard, early in BR days. Aside from an enlarged casing on the (far) right-hand side and the boiler, the obvious visual change was the smoke deflectors, fitted in July 1939 to combat drifting smoke. The Timken roller bearings fitted to coupled wheels and the tender were not obvious but it is possible (I'm told) to discern differences in the ventilator louvres on the casings over time. A typical entry concerning the engine's last years comes in *The Railway Observer* of January 1950. On 15 December the previous year, it recorded, the 'Turbo' had lost time all the way from Euston with the 8.30am Liverpool train, and had to be taken off at Rugby and replaced by a Black Five. 46202 later made its sad way north (presumably for Crewe) behind an ex-LNW 0-8-0. Photograph Jim Davenport.

Outside cylinders – cast iron 'Coronation'
Coupled wheels – originals but machined and rebalanced
Motion – new, 'Coronation' type
Main frames – new, 'Coronation' type modified at front end
Smokebox and fittings – all new
Cab – original, modified to take reversing gear
Boiler mountings – new superheater header and elements.'

Costing nearly £9,000 to convert, the new locomotive went into traffic on 15 August 1952; as is well known, the eventful story of this particular Pacific came to a horribly violent end at Harrow & Wealdstone only weeks later, on 8 October. The remains were taken away and finally officially condemned at Crewe in May 1954.

*** ***

The Turbo was, in the end, quite a commendable machine and was probably the best of the experimental 'one-offs'. It performed far more useful work, for instance, than Paget's 2-6-2, FURY, the LNER 'Hush-Hush' or the SR Leader (the latter expanded, nominally, to five locomotives).

6202's problems were certainly not improved by fitters' unfamiliarity at sheds, though a fitter always travelled with the engine – 'Tiggy' Brearton, a Crewe man – did the job for years, it is said. Standing on shed, however, making an odd sound perhaps, or refusing to move, the Turbo could thoroughly perplex whoever had the job (and was cursing his luck) that particular shift, at Camden or Edge Hill. No one else would touch it of course and whenever it failed it would never be 'fixed up' at some local shed the

way any other main line failure would be. It was always towed away to Crewe Works, Liverpool or London. It has been recorded that days were sometimes wasted stripping down parts only to find, in the end, nothing amiss. A larger class, affording everyday experience of Turbo foibles would have enjoyed the benefit of spares off the shelf; with more enthusiasm and confidence might we have seen a class of super-turbos and not the Coronations?

Unlikely, yet 6202 could at least equal, and excel on occasion, the performance of one of her conventional sisters when all went well. On the credit side it delivered no hammer blow, firebox maintenance was low on account of the even exhaust and frame maintenance should have been reduced with the steady torque of the turbine drive. It was not to be.

It is not surprising that few photographs survive of PRINCESS ANNE at work, though here it is at Shrewsbury in those brief eight weeks. It should have received an open footplate in front of the cylinders but in the event was turned out with proper 'Lizzie' style curved fronts. The boiler was that previously used in its turbine life and another departure was the change in footplate level in the region of the trailing coupled wheel. The tender was the first of this most familiar Stanier type, despite slight differences at the back steps and seems to have been destroyed at Harrow too. It ran with the loco throughout its life; the 'Turbo' never ran with a high sided ten ton tender.

The first of the 'standard' batch, the ten which formed a main plank of the 1935 Building Programme. Construction of the Princess Royals was terminated in favour of the bigger Coronations and with the 'Turbo' the class remained, unluckily, at just thirteen. 46203 PRINCESS MARGARET ROSE is on good form, roaring past Bourne End signals at something like 65mph, a little after noon on 25 March 1950, with the up 8.15am express from Liverpool Lime Street. The livery is still LMS black, though with plain letters on the tender and BR numbering on the engine. Photograph E.D. Bruton.

MORE PRINCESSES

'...certain modifications have been made as dictated by experience gained with their prototypes.'
The Locomotive, 15 August 1935.

46203 at Polmadie, its home in the early 1950s – photograph taken between 3/52 (green livery) and 8/58 (second BR crest). Photograph B.P. Hoper Collection.

With all that was learned from its first Pacifics, a year later ten more were approved, suitably modified in the light of experience. They were to be part of the 1935 Programme, two years after the first ones appeared – so the provision of big new express engines for the upgrading of the West Coast working could hardly be compared to the Royal Scots' hurried introduction, for instance. The 1935 scheme of new building, promulgated in 1934, was concerned principally with new mixed traffic 4-6-0s

and new passenger tanks; the extract below is the part which included the new Princesses.

6203 was the first of the 'new Princesses' and it appeared in July 1935; two more followed later in the month another four in August, two in September and the final one in October 1935. By 1935, streamlining was in the air, if that faint echo of a pun can be forgiven, but fortunately the Princesses were too far advanced for an early wind tunnel-derived arrangement to be fitted.

Fortunately the world was spared a streamlined Princess, though the special cowl of the outline drawing of 1934, reproduced earlier, is a curious survival of the thinking of the day.

The new batch had higher sided tenders from the first, and all the boilers were obviously different. 6203-6212 had shorter barrels and lengthened fireboxes, bringing forward the joint between barrel and firebox to a point over the centre of the trailing driving wheel. The alteration in size was made by extending the firebox forward to form a larger combustion chamber. The barrel rings were different, there were minor frame changes to accommodate the differences and hollow axles (as on the GWR King) were used. The need for enhanced superheat had been known, but of the ten boilers the first four had twenty-four elements, not the optimum thirty-two, though they all later got the higher number.

The steam pipes to the inside cylinders, in the smokebox, were altered (later 6200 and 6201 got the same arrangement); the chimneys were different and so were the slidebars. These were to a more familiar LMS pattern and did not have the GWR look of those fitted to 6200 and 6201. The motion brackets on 6200-6212 were different too, passing outside the slidebars as opposed to the earlier arrangement which took the motion bracket behind the slidebars. The motion pins of the valve gear took advantage of up-to-date practice, having roller bearings; the exceptions were the driving bearings of the outside eccentric rods, which had 'Skefko' double row self-align-

```
                                        27th June, 1934.

Locomotive Renewal Programme, 1935.  N.W.O. 3460.

                    Submitted, with the approval of the
Executive Committee, report (June 1934) from the Chief Mechanical
Engineer, the Chief Operating Manager and the Chief Accountant
addressed to the Traffic and the Mechanical & Electrical Engineering
Committees recommending that during 1935 the following new loco-
motives be constructed to meet traffic requirements and in replace-
ment of locomotives to be displaced and broken up :-

                          New Locomotives            Locomotives to be
                          to be built.               displaced.

                      No.   Cost of             No.    Replacement
                            Engines and                Cost.
                            Tenders.
                            £.                          £.
LOCOMOTIVES.

Tender - Passenger.

(a)  Princess Royal
     Class 7 (4-6-2).  10     107,000.

(b)  Class 5X (4-6-0)  30     192,000.

(c)  Mixed Traffic
     Class 5 (4-6-0)   55     338,250.

                       95     637,250.       64      278,209.
```

ing radial ball bearings. The trailing Bissel trucks of five of the engines had roller bearings, and five plain bearings – though which five were which remains unclear.

The mechanical lubricators were re-arranged; whereas the earlier two Pacifics had one each side, the new batch had one on the left-hand and two on the right-hand side. The extra one seems to have been for the coupled axleboxes

The extended firebox necessitated a new reversing gear rod, with differences that are clear in pictures. There were other changes, most of them (hopefully) illustrated and described in the 'engine picking' captions.

A Complication of Boilers
To most at the time, in the middle 1930s, the new Princesses were effectively identical to their two predecessors, and one of the few differences a respected journal such as *The Locomotive* felt drawn to comment upon was the new tenders –

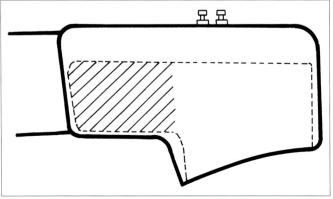

Hatched volume was the combustion chamber, not normally present on a narrow firebox loco. It was the volume contained between the tubeplate and the front of the firegrate.

'larger than the ones fitted to the two earlier engines'. The principal changes of course, were in the firebox heating surface and, far more tellingly, the very considerable increase in the superheating.

Stanier had brought a number of Swindon-style features to his work on the LMS and while many were completely successful and merely absorbed into LMS practice, others were modified, improved, or abandoned according to experience. The taper boiler would be a classic example of a successful innovation, while the imported notion of low superheat would not work on bigger engines with different coal (of lower BTUs), driven by men with a different tradition.

The Swindon model of regulator working in the superheater header, in the smokebox, was something that could not be made to give satisfaction on the LMS, and it was of course one feature that characterised the first Pacifics. Eventually, by the 1950s, the regulator in all the boilers was placed in a dome on the boiler and full interchangeability was at last established. The question of what changes occurred to what boilers, and the engines for which they could serve is a hopelessly complicated one, even for so small a class and the accompanying boiler tables, compiled at such length by Peter Rowledge and

kindly made available for the first time here, cover the 'phases' of 'Lizzie' boiler life. It is in theory possible to *write* the story of the Princess boilers chronologically but it soon becomes very hard to follow, if indeed this particular author was up to the task of putting it into some simple form.

As a matter of definition, 'domeless' does not necessarily mean the *absence* of a dome shaped cover on the boiler (bear with me). 'Domeless' means that the there is no raised dome to collect steam *for the regulator underneath*, though there might well be a dome for the top feed. 'Domed' means that the dome *actually* contains a regulator. This combination of features had a continuous bearing on the look of the Princess Royals.

This definition is about right, but perhaps mention should be made of where the steam comes from when there *isn't* a dome. Steam has to be collected from the highest point within the boiler, to avoid 'carry-over' of water into the cylinders, with consequent disastrous results to cylinder covers and so on. Boilers got larger and larger in diameter and still had to be within the loading gauge, so alternatives to a dome were explored – the 'steam collector' of the 'Lizzies' for instance, was first placed just ahead of the firebox, as high as possible – that is, it was within the main boiler shell. From here the collected steam passed to the combined superheater header and regulator valve within the smokebox. Top feeds could certainly *look* like 'domes' but inside there wasn't really any room for anything more than the top feed apparatus itself. One great advantage of a conventional dome for steam collection, however, rather than the 'steam collector' and regulator valve in the smokebox was ease

Official works record of 6205 PRINCESS VICTORIA, showing the exquisite neatness of line which characterised these locomotives. This is the original livery of course, a striking crimson lake, or 'red' if you prefer, with twelve inch gold characters shaded in black and letter spacing at five feet. Note original standard nine ton Stanier tender, far less flamboyant than the swept-up ten tonners; also vacuum pump on crosshead – these were removed from 1938. This side-on view is a good illustration of the 'long firebox', extending to the mid-point of the rear splasher.

of maintenance. A smokebox was an appalling place to work after all.

BOILER 'PHASES'

The accompanying tables of 'details of boilers fitted' begin with 46200 on page 32. They show much detail and through a lifetime's study which even the term 'monastic devotion' fails to convey adequately, Peter Rowledge has wrought these data (there – the word I swore to avoid in these books) into 'Phases' in the lives of these boilers. For this and other kindnesses in this series of books I am exceedingly grateful.

New Front Ends

Eight of the Princesses got new front end frames, as follows:
46200 - 2/52
46201 - 3/52
46203 - 3/52
46205 - 9/52
46206 - 8/53
46207 - 1/54
46210 - 3/53
46211 - 12/52

46203 was actually done at Derby, which was the only time an LMS Pacific was shopped there. The engines got com-

Tender	Built	Type	Loco	From	To
9000	27/06/33	9ton riv.	6200	27/06/33	05/06/35
9001	03/11/33	9ton riv.	6201	03/11/33	12/06/35
9003	29/06/35	9ton riv.	6202	29/06/35	U.W.
9065	09/05/35	9ton riv.	6200	09/05/35	20/06/36
			6201	20/06/36	09/12/36
9066	28/03/35	9ton riv.	6201	28/03/35	20/06/36
			6200	20/06/36	30/11/36
9124	01/07/35	9ton riv.	6203	01/07/35	23/12/36
9125	19/07/35	9ton riv.	6204	19/07/35	29/12/36
9126	24/07/35	9ton riv.	6205	24/07/35	28/05/36
9127	01/08/35	9ton riv.	6206	01/08/35	24/09/36
9128	09/08/35	9ton riv.	6207	09/08/35	31/12/36
9129	16/08/35	9ton riv.	6208	16/08/35	24/07/36
9130	23/08/35	9ton riv.	6209	23/08/35	09/10/36
9131	06/09/35	9ton riv.	6210	06/09/35	03/10/36
9132	15/09/35	9ton riv.	6211	15/09/35	02/07/36
9133	19/10/35	9ton riv.	6212	19/06/35	07/08/36
9344*	29/05/36	9ton riv. H.S.	6205	29/05/36	17/07/36
			6208	03/07/36	11/03/37
			6205	11/03/37	25/11/61
9345*	29/06/36	9ton riv. H.S.	6211	29/06/36	07/10/61
			6212	05/12/44	4/62
9353*	17/07/36	9ton riv. H.S.	6205	17/07/36	11/03/37
			6208	11/03/37	16/06/39
			6210	16/06/39	25/12/39
			6207	25/12/39	20/11/46
			6206	20/11/46	17/10/47
			6207	17/10/47	25/11/61
9354*	28/07/36	9ton riv. H.S.	6212	28/07/36	05/12/44
			6211	05/12/44	04/09/46
			6209	04/09/46	29/09/62
9359*	15/10/36	9ton riv. H.S.	6206	15/10/36	20/11/46
			6207	20/11/46	17/10/47
			6206	17/10/47	18/10/62
			6221	18/10/62	18/05/63
9360*	25/09/36	9ton riv. H.S.	6210	25/09/36	16/06/39
			6208	16/06/39	03/11/62
9361*	01/10/36	9ton riv. H.S.	6209	01/10/36	04/09/46
			6211	04/09/46	07/10/61
9372*	06/11/36	9ton riv. H.S.	6200	06/11/36	13/08/55
			6210	13/08/55	07/10/61
9373*	28/11/36	9ton riv. H.S.	6201	28/11/36	20/10/62
9374*	19/01/37	9ton riv. H.S.	6203	19/01/37	03/11/62
9375*	19/12/36	9ton riv. H.S.	6204	19/12/36	07/10/61
9376*	18/12/36	9ton riv. H.S.	6207	18/12/36	20/12/39
			6210	20/12/39	11/08/55
			6200	27/08/55	01/12/62
9816		10ton welded Duchess tender	6206	18/10/62	03/11/62

9ton riv. = 9ton riveted
9 ton riv. H.S. = 9ton riveted High Sided
U.W. = Until Withdrawal
* = Classified to 10 ton 25/12/37
Details are largely from those worked on from Tender Record Cards by Brassmasters – send for a catalogue of their fine LMS 4mm kits: PO Box 1137, Sutton Coldfield, West Midlands, B76 1FU.
The details tie in with the Engine Cards well enough and I think it fairly complete now – though any errors are mine alone!

pletely new sections of frame, along with new inside cylinders; the work seems to have been done as and when it was found necessary. Some simply 'wore' better than others and such renewal work was never necessary. There had always been a tendency for the outside cylinders to work a bit loose – a deficiency which was said to result from the cylinders being positioned over the trailing wheels of the bogie. The problem was always present in some degree, and 'shear strips' were welded on to the frames. This apparently was carried out later in the 1950s, to all the engines, though 46203 at least got them at

the same time as the new frames and inside cylinders. The purpose of the 'shear strips' was to provide an indication of cylinder movement; they were welded on with the cylinder removed with all bolt holes filled. New bolt holes were drilled out and the face of the 'shear strip' machined for refitting of the cylinder. Movement was betrayed by cracking along the weld.

6205 PRINCESS VICTORIA

In 1938 PRINCESS VICTORIA had the two inside sets of Walshaerts valve gear removed and rocking levers substituted.

A roaring exit from Glasgow Central Platform 3, as 46206 leaves with the 10.5am to Birmingham on 28 May 1959. Photograph R.C. Riley.

These were located between the front of the outside steamchests and the rear of the inside ones, so that the outside motion worked the valves of the inside cylinders. The resulting motion brackets were like nothing seen elsewhere and are quite unmistakable in pictures. By May 1941, it was determined that the effort and expense had been 'worthwhile' but, significantly, there was no suggestion that any other Princesses be so altered.

TENDER TALE

It will come as no surprise that the tale of the Princess tenders, despite it being such a small class, is not a simple one... 6200 and 6201 began their careers with straight sided tenders that looked much like the familiar Fowler ones already fitted to so many engines. These were much bigger however, carrying nine tons of coal and 4,000 gallons of water, on a wheelbase of fifteen feet – two feet more than the earlier versions. The design was not 'new' in the sense that the drawings had already been worked out so they were, in a way, 'off the peg'. Yet they were 'new' in that they were *not* a modified version of earlier Derby-type tenders, as fitted to the Crabs and so on; they were wider and longer than the earlier 'Fowler' ones. Three were built, 9000-9002, to fit Princesses 6200-6202; 9000 and 9002 had roller bearings and with 6202 (the Turbomotive) not ready Stanier was somewhat relieved to be able to pinch roller bearing tender 9002 for ROYAL SCOT's American tour.

Apart from not looking very nice (in particular they did not complement the engines aesthetically at all) tenders 9000-9002 did not 'behave' well, in that self-trimming did not work in the right way. Stanier reported that *'it was desirable to obtain a better self-trimming type*

46200 THE PRINCESS ROYAL

DATE	DETAILS OF BOILERS FITTED													
	No.	Position of regulator	Comb. Chamber Fitted or not	Length Between Tube Plates	Large Tubes No.	Large Tubes Outs dia (ins)	Small Tubes No.	Small Tubes Outs dia (ins)	HEATING SURFACE (SQ FT) Fire-box	Tubes	Element	Total	PHASE (SEE NOTES)	
5/33	6048	HEADER	NO	20'9"	16	5⅛	168	2¼	190	2523	370	3083	1	A
4/35	6050	HEADER	NO	20'9"	32	5⅛	110	2¼	190	2240	623	3053	2	B
11/36	-	-	-	-	-	-	-	-	-	-	-	-	-	C
5/37	6049	DOME	NO	20'9"	32	5⅛	119	2⅜	190	2425	623	3238	6	
8/39	6048	DOME	NO	20'9"	32	5⅛	119	2⅜	190	2425	623	3238	6	
4/42	6050	HEADER	NO	20'9"	32	5⅛	110	2⅜	190	2310	623	3123	2	
10/44	6048	DOME	NO	20'9"	32	5⅛	119	2⅜	190	2425	623	3238	6	
8/47	6050	HEADER	NO	20'9"	32	5⅛	110	2⅜	190	2310	623	3123	2	
7/48	6048	DOME	NO	20'9"	32	5⅛	119	2⅜	190	2425	623	3238	6	
1/52	9106	HEADER	YES	19'3"	32	5⅛	123	2⅜	217	2299	623	3139	8	D
9/56	9103	DOME	YES	19'3"	32	5⅛	123	2⅜	217	2299	623	3139	9	E

A The motion followed GW practice in appearance eg large slidebars, inclined at the ends to clear the connecting rod and eccentric rods attached to a pin on the side of the expansion link. A vacuum pump was fitted driven off the LH crosshead and attached to the LH bottom slidebar. The reversing gear bridle rod was in two parts connected through an intermediate lever carried on a bracket attached to the main frame 1ft.9¼in. to rear of the trailing coupled wheel. There was no steady bracket for the bridle rod.
The tender (9000) was of Fowler design in appearance but was wider and carried 4000 gallons water. It was carried on roller bearings.
B Tender 9000 replaced by tender 9065 of standard 9 ton, 4000 gallon design.
C Tender 9065 replaced by tender 9372 of 10 ton capacity standard design (riveted).
D In order to accommodate boilers 9100-9109, 9235 and 9236, a hole had to be cut in the lagging on the throatplate to clear the inside arm of the reversing gear bridle rod intermediate lever. When this was agreed boilers 6048-50 became available to the rest of the class. In addition some modifications were required to the ashpan when these boilers were exchanged.
E The engine was fitted with steam operated cylinder cocks.

ENGINE 46201 PRINCESS ELIZABETH

DATE	DETAILS OF BOILERS FITTED								HEATING SURFACE (SQ FT)				PHASE (SEE NOTES)	
	No.	Position of regulator	Comb. Chamber Fitted or not	Length Between Tube Plates	Large Tubes No.	Outs dia (ins)	Small Tubes No.	Outs dia (ins)	Fire-box	Tubes	Element	Total		
8/33	6049	HEADER	NO	20'9"	16	5⅛	168	2¼	190	2523	370	3083	1	A
3/35	-	-	-	-	-	-	-	-	-	-	-	-	-	B
10/35	6048	DOME	NO	20'9"	32	5⅛	119	2⅜	190	2425	623	3238	6	
11/36	-	-	-	-	-	-	-	-	-	-	-	-	-	C
9/37	6050	HEADER	NO	20'9"	32	5⅛	110	2¼	190	2240	623	3053	2	
2/40	6049	DOME	NO	20'9"	32	5⅛	119	2⅜	190	2425	623	3238	6	
9/42	6048	DOME	NO	20'9"	32	5⅛	119	2⅜	190	2425	623	3238	6	
6/44	6-49	DOME	NO	20'9"	32	5⅛	119	2⅜	190	2425	623	3238	6	
11/45	6050	HEADER	NO	20'9"	32	5⅛	110	2⅜	190	2310	623	3123	2	
7/46	6049	DOME	NO	20'9"	32	5⅛	119	2⅜	190	2425	623	3238	6	
11/48	6050	HEADER	NO	20'9"	32	5⅛	110	2⅜	190	2310	623	3123	2	
2/52	9109	HEADER	YES	19'3"	32	5⅛	123	2⅜	217	2299	623	3139	8	D
7/54	9103	DOME	YES	19'3"	32	5⅛	123	2⅜	217	2299	623	3139	9	
4/56	9235	DOME	YES	19'3"	32	5⅛	123	2⅜	217	2299	623	3139	9	E

A   The engine was identical with 6200 in all respects. Tender fitted was 9001 Fowler type but wider. Capacity 4000 gallons; carried on roller bearings.

B   Tender 9001 replaced by tender 9066 of standard 9 ton, 4000 gallon capacities.

C   Tender 9066 replaced by tender 9373 of standard 10 ton capacity (riveted).

D   The same modifications to the lagging were required as are noted under engine 6200.

E   The engine was fitted with steam operated cylinder cocks.

of coal bunker and to provide better facilities for carrying fire irons, etc.'. The original straight sided tenders were soon replaced by the now familiar 'standard' Stanier sloping sided form, so that 6200 and 6201 got new tenders 9065 and 9066 in April and March 1935; 6202 (the 'Turbo') also got one, 9003, from new in June 1935. So it was that only 6200 and 6201, the first two Pacifics, ran with the unflattering straight sided tenders. All three – the two on the Pacifics and the one which went to America with ROYAL SCOT – soon disappeared, rebuilt (under an Order of 25 October 1935, at an authorised cost of £505) into the now

standard Stanier sloping sided form and given to new Class 5 4-6-0s. The new batch of Pacifics, 6203-6212, got these new-style riveted Stanier tenders, and looked much better for it.

These tenders were replaced from mid-1936 onwards by the familiar high sided type, still riveted (unlike the Duchess tanks which were welded) though at first they were also of a nominal nine ton capacity. Pacifics of course, were running longer distances than had been customary and even at nine tons, the capacity was found to be limited. They were uprated in late 1937 to ten tonners; they were attached to all the Princesses ex-

cept the Turbomotive, which kept a standard style of tender even after rebuilding into conventional form.

The 'sieve boxes' which were developed as standard features from the late 1940s, also appeared on the Princess tenders. This was an external feed system, which largely did away for the need to clamber inside the tank and sort out blockages. In this new way of doing things all that was required was to clean a sieve inside the box; a disadvantage was the exposed position outside on the tender framing, where they could freeze solid in winter.

One ten tonner, presumably anticipating later developments with the Corona-

PRINCESS MARGARET ROSE, with 66A Polmadie shedplate, stands in Carnforth shed yard some time in the 1950s – the tender still bears the first style of emblem. It was here that some Lizzies were later to end up, stored. Photograph Canon A. George, B.P. Hoper Collection.

ENGINE 46202 PRINCESS ANNE (NAMED 1952)

DATE	DETAILS OF BOILERS FITTED				Large Tubes		Small Tubes		HEATING SURFACE (SQ FT)				PHASE (SEE NOTES)	
	No.	Position of regulator	Comb. Chamber Fitted Or not	Length Between Tube Plates	No.	Outs dia (ins)	No.	Outs dia (ins)	Fire-box	Tubes	Element	Total		
6/35	9100	HEADER	YES	19'3"	32	5⅛	112	2⅜	217	2167	623	3007	3	A
7/36	9236	DOME	YES	19'3"	40	5⅛	81	2¼	217	1951	540	2708	7	
10/37														B
2/39														C
9/39 to 7/41														D
7/43														E
9/44	9236	DOME	YES	19'3"	40	5⅛	81	2¼	217	1951	832	3000	7	
12/46	9236	DOME	YES	19'3"	40	5⅛	81	2¼	217	1951	832	3000	7	
8/50														F
7/52	9236	DOME	YES	19'3"	40	5⅛	101	2⅜	217	2232	720	3169	10	G
9/52														H

A   The engine differed in appearance from all the other Princess Royal locomotives due to the adoption of turbine propulsion. The forward turbine was on the LH side roughly in the position normally occupied by the cylinder and the reverse turbine was in a similar position on the RH side. Steam inlet valves occupied the casings on each side of the smokebox and on the LH side a casing extended to the cab, concealing pumps, control rods etc. The tender fitted was 9003 of standard 9 ton and 4000 gallon capacity.

B   Ventilation louvres added to turbine casings.

C   Smoke deflectors fitted.

D   Engine stored, paint shop Crewe Works.

E   Engine stopped due to failure of flexible drive. Boiler removed and fitted to 6210.

F   Engine withdrawn from service. Boiler removed and fitted to 46204.

G   Engine converted to 4 cylinders reciprocating propulsion; using Duchess cylinders 16½" x 28" rocking levers to inside valves, single chimney. (Tractive effort becomes 41,5000lb).

H   Following extensive damage in the Harrow accident the engine was cut up and replaced by 71000. Boiler retained.

---

tion Pacifics, had a steam operated coal pusher; this was 9359 attached to 6206 PRINCESS MARIE LOUISE and could only work when fitted to that locomotive. Accordingly, the two were hardly ever separated from one another. The odd 'swop' of riveted and welded tenders between 46206 and Coronation 46221 late in 1962 may have been to give the latter a coal pusher tender while its own was under repair – in any case it seems to have been only a short-lived 'paper' transfer before the Princess was withdrawn a few weeks later. Certainly no photographs have come to light with 46221 hauling this riveted tender.

Vacuum Pumps

The Princesses when built had vacuum pumps worked off the outside left-hand crossheads, just as the first Royal Scots, but all were removed as not worth the maintenance from 1938.

Black-liveried PRINCESS MARIE LOUISE leaves the double track bore of Northchurch Tunnel, just to the north of Berkhamsted, with the down 4.30pm Euston to Liverpool Lime Street, 2 September 1950. Photograph E.D. Bruton.

ENGINE 46203 PRINCESS MARGARET ROSE

DATE	DETAILS OF BOILERS FITTED					Large Tubes		Small Tubes		HEATING SURFACE (SQ FT)				PHASE (SEE NOTES)	
	No.	Position of regulator	Comb. Chamber Fitted or not	Length Between Tube Plates		No.	Outs dia (ins)	No.	Outs dia (ins)	Fire-Box	Tubes	Element	Total		
7/35	9101	HEADER	YES	19'3"		24	5⅛	141	2⅜	217	2308	467	2992	4	A
12/36	9100	HEADER	YES	19'3"		32	5⅛	112	2⅜	217	2167	623	3007	3	B
11/38	9101	HEADER	YES	19'3"		24	5⅛	141	2⅜	217	2308	467	2992	4	
11/41	9106	HEADER	YES	19'3"		32	5⅛	112	2⅜	217	2167	623	3007	3	
6/44	9102	HEADER	YES	19'3"		24	5⅛	141	2⅜	217	2308	467	2992	4	
10/47	9106	HEADER	YES	19'3"		32	5⅛	123	2⅜	217	2299	623	3139	8	
4/51	9108	HEADER	YES	19'3"		32	5⅛	123	2⅜	217	2299	623	3139	8	
9/55	9101	DOME	YES	19'3"		32	5⅛	123	2⅜	217	2299	623	3139	9	
6/58	9100	DOME	YES	19'3"		32	5⅛	112	2⅜	217	2167	623	3007	9A	C

A   Although similar to 6200/01 in general appearance there were a number of detail differences. The slidebars were shorter without 'flared' ends, the eccentric rods was attached to a downward and backward extension of the expansion link; a vacuum pump was fitted in the same position as on 6200/01. The reversing gear bridle rod was in two parts connected through an intermediate lever mounted 1' 9½" in front of the trailing coupled wheel. A steady bracket for the rear half bridle rod was provided 3'8½" to the rear of the trailing coupled wheel and inset into the firebox lagging. The tender was 9124 of standard 9 ton and 4000 gallons capacity.

B   Tender 9124 replaced by tender 9374 of 10 ton capacity.

C   The engine was fitted with steam operated cylinder cocks.

ENGINE 46204 PRINCESS LOUISE

DATE	DETAILS OF BOILERS FITTED					Large Tubes		Small Tubes		HEATING SURFACE (SQ FT)				PHASE (SEE NOTES)	
	No.	Position of regulator	Comb. Chamber Fitted or not	Length Between Tube Plates		No.	Outs dia (ins)	No.	Outs dia (ins)	Fire-box	Tubes	Element	Total		
9/35	9102	HEADER	YES	19'3"		24	5⅛	141	2⅜	217	2308	467	2992	4	A
10/37	9105	HEADER	YES	19'3"		32	5⅛	112	2⅜	217	2167	623	3007	3	B
9/40	9109	HEADER	YES	19'3"		32	5⅛	112	2⅜	217	2167	623	3007	3	
5/44	9103	HEADER	YES	19'3"		32	5⅛	123	2⅜	217	2299	623	3139	8	
9/46	9108	HEADER	YES	19'3"		32	5⅛	112	2⅜	217	2167	623	3007	3	
8/50	9236	DOME	YES	19'3"		40	5⅛	81	2¼	217	1951	832	3000	7	
5/52	6048	DOME	NO	20'9"		32	5⅛	119	2⅜	190	2424	623	3237	6	
5/55	6049	DOME	NO	20'9"		32	5⅛	119	2⅜	190	2424	623	3237	6	
8/58	6049	DOME	NO	20'9"		32	5⅛	119	2⅜	190	2424	623	3237	6	

A   The engine was identical with 6203. The tender fitted was 9125 of standard 9 ton, 4000 gallon design.

B   Tender 9125 replaced by tender 9375 of 10 ton capacity.

PRINCESS ARTHUR OF CONNAUGHT in red livery, in Crewe Works yard, 1935. The Princesses were never entirely eclipsed on the London-Crewe-Perth runs; the Liverpool trains remained a stronghold, while the Holyhead line saw them at whiles. 6207 was one of five sent to Longsight for a few months in 1939, working to London via Crewe – they were barred from the Stoke line, which made them awkward so far as Longsight was concerned. This was doubtless the reason that Princesses did not become a fixture at Manchester.

ENGINE 46205 PRINCESS VICTORIA

DATE	No.	Position of regulator	Comb. Chamber Fitted or not	Length Between Tube Plates	Large Tubes No.	Outs dia (ins)	Small Tubes No.	Outs dia (ins)	Fire-Box	Tubes	Element	Total	PHASE	(SEE NOTES)
9/35	9103	HEADER	YES	19'3"	24	5⅛	141	2⅜	217	2308	467	2992	4	A
1936	-	-	-	-	-	-	-	-	-	-	-	-	-	B
3/38	9103	HEADER	YES	19'3"	24	5⅛	141	2⅜	217	2308	467	2992	4	C
1/41	9108	HEADER	YES	19'3"	32	5⅛	112	2⅜	217	2167	623	3007	3	
10/42	9104	HEADER	YES	19'3"	24	5⅛	141	2⅜	217	2308	467	2992	4	
1/45	9109	HEADER	YES	19'3"	32	5⅛	123	2⅜	217	2299	623	3139	8	
9/48	9235	DOME	YES	19'3"	32	5⅛	112	2⅜	217	2167	623	3007	5	
7/52	9105	DOME	YES	19'3"	32	5⅛	112	2⅜	217	2167	623	3007	9A	
1/56	9107	DOME	YES	19'3"	32	5⅛	123	2⅜	217	2299	623	3139	9	
8/58	9109	DOME	YES	19'3"	32	5⅛	123	2⅜	217	2299	623	3139	9	

A   The engine was identical with 6203. The tender fitted was No 9126 of standard 9 ton and 4000 gallon design.
B   Tender 9126 replaced by tender 9353 of 10 ton capacity.
C   Inside motion removed and inside valves driven by rocking levers ahead of outside cylinders.

ENGINE 46206 PRINCESS MARIE LOUISE

DATE	No.	Position of regulator	Comb. Chamber Fitted or not	Length Between Tube Plates	Large Tubes No.	Outs dia (ins)	Small Tubes No.	Outs dia (ins)	Fire-Box	Tubes	Element	Total	PHASE	(SEE NOTES)
9/35	9104	HEADER	19'3"	24	24	5⅛	141	2⅜	217	2308	467	2992	4	A
10/36	-	-	-	-	-	-	-	-	-	-	-	-	-	B
7/37	9235	DOME	19'3"	32	32	5⅛	112	2⅜	217	2167	623	3007	5	
6/39	9100	HEADER	19'3"	32	32	5⅛	112	2⅜	217	2167	623	3007	3	
11/42	9108	HEADER	19'3"	32	32	5⅛	112	2⅜	217	2167	623	3007	3	
8/43	9235	DOME	19'3"	32	32	5⅛	112	2⅜	217	2167	623	3007	5	
7/45	9104	HEADER	19'3"	24	24	5⅛	141	2⅜	217	2308	467	2992	4	
1/48	9102	HEADER	19'3"	24	24	5⅛	141	2⅜	217	2308	467	2992	4	
9/50	9101	HEADER	19'3"	32	32	5⅛	123	2⅜	217	2299	623	3139	8	
2/55	9100	DOME	19'3"	32	32	5⅛	123	2⅜	217	2299	623	3139	9	
1/58	9105	DOME	19'3"	32	32	5⅛	112	2⅜	217	2167	623	3007	9	C

A   The engine was identical with 6203. The tender fitted was 9127 of 9 ton, 4000 gallon design.
B   Tender 9127 replaced by tender 9359 of 10 ton capacity – fitted with a coal pusher.
C   The engine was fitted with steam operated cylinder cocks.

ENGINE 46207 PRINCESS ARTHUR OF CONNAUGHT

DATE	No.	Position of regulator	Comb. Chamber Fitted or not	Length Between Tube Plates	Large Tubes No.	Outs dia (ins)	Small Tubes No.	Outs dia (ins)	Fire-Box	Tubes	Element	Total	PHASE	(SEE NOTES)
9/35	9105	HEADER	YES	19'3"	32	5⅛	112	2⅜	217	2167	623	3007	3	A
12/36	-	-	-	-	-	-	-	-	-	-	-	-	-	B
8/37	9104	HEADER	YES	19'3"	24	5⅛	141	2⅜	217	2308	467	2992	4	
1/40	9102	HEADER	YES	19'3"	24	5⅛	141	2⅜	217	2308	467	2992	4	
12/41	9101	HEADER	YES	19'3"	24	5⅛	141	2⅜	217	2308	467	2992	4	
11/43	9108	HEADER	YES	19'3"	32	5⅛	112	2⅜	217	2167	623	3007	3	
5/46	9100	HEADER	YES	19'3"	32	5⅛	112	2⅜	217	2167	623	3007	3	
3/49	9105	HEADER	YES	19'3"	32	5⅛	112	2⅜	217	2167	623	3007	3	
11/51	9102	HEADER	YES	19'3"	32	5⅛	123	2⅜	217	2299	623	3139	8	
11/55	9109	DOME	YES	19'3"	32	5⅛	123	2⅜	217	2299	623	3139	9	
3/58	9106	DOME	YES	19'3"	32	5⅛	123	2⅜	217	2299	623	3139	9	C

A   The engine was identical with 6203. The tender fitted was 9128 of 9 ton, 4000 gallons standard design.
B   Tender 9128 replaced by tender 9376 of 10 ton capacity.
C   The engine was fitted with steam operated cylinder cocks.

ENGINE 46208 PRINCESS HELENA VICTORIA

DATE	No.	Position of regulator	Comb. Chamber Fitted or not	Length Between Tube Plates	Large Tubes No.	Outs dia (ins)	Small Tubes No.	Outs dia (ins)	Fire-Box	Tubes	Element	Total	PHASE	(SEE NOTES)
9/35	9106	HEADER	YES	19'3"	32	5⅛	112	2⅜	217	2167	623	3007	3	A
7/36	-	-	-	-	-	-	-	-	-	-	-	-	-	B
4/37	9106	HEADER	YES	19'3"	32	5⅛	112	2⅜	217	2167	623	3007	3	
4/38	9109	HEADER	YES	19'3"	32	5⅛	112	2⅜	217	2167	623	3007	3	
4/40	9104	HEADER	YES	19'3"	24	5⅛	141	2⅜	217	2308	467	2992	4	
9/42	9107	HEADER	YES	19'3"	32	5⅛	112	2⅜	217	2167	623	3007	3	
9/46	9235	DOME	YES	19'3"	32	5⅛	112	2⅜	217	2167	623	3007	5	
3/48	9104	HEADER	YES	19'3"	24	5⅛	141	2⅜	217	2308	467	2992	4	
8/50	6049	DOME	NO	20'9"	32	5⅛	119	2⅜	190	2425	623	3238	6	
10/52	6050	DOME	NO	20'9"	32	5⅛	110	2⅜	190	2310	623	3123	2	
2/57	9104	DOME	YES	19'3"	32	5⅛	123	2⅜	217	2299	623	3139	9	C
9/58	9104	DOME	YES	19'3"	32	5⅛	123	2⅜	217	2299	623	3139	9	

A   The engine was identical with 6203. The tender fitted was 9129 of 9 tons, 4000 gallons standard design.
B   Tender 9129 replaced by tender 9344 of 10 ton capacity.
C   The engine was fitted with steam operated cylinder cocks.

ENGINE 46209 PRINCESS BEATRICE

DATE	DETAILS OF BOILERS FITTED No.	Position of regu- lator	Comb. Cham- ber Fitted or not	Length Between Tube Plates	Large Tubes No.	Outs dia (ins)	Small Tubes No.	Outs dia (ins)	HEATING SURFACE (SQ FT) Fire- Box	Tubes	Element	Total	PHASE (SEE NOTES)	
9/35	9107	HEADER	YES	19'3"	32	5⅛	112	2⅜	217	2167	623	3007	3	A
10/36	-	-	-	-	-	-	-	-	-	-	-	-	-	B
2/37	9101	HEADER	YES	19'3"	24	5⅛	141	2⅜	217	2308	467	2992	4	
10/38	9106	HEADER	YES	19'3"	32	5⅛	112	2⅜	217	2167	623	3007	3	
7/41	9103	HEADER	YES	19'3"	24	5⅛	141	2⅜	217	2308	467	2992	4	
11/43	9105	HEADER	YES	19'3"	32	5⅛	112	2⅜	217	2167	623	3007	3	
11/45	9107	HEADER	YES	19'3"	32	5⅛	123	2⅜	217	2299	623	3139	8	
11/48	9109	HEADER	YES	19'3"	32	5⅛	123	2⅜	217	2299	623	3139	8	
8/51	9104	HEADER	YES	19'3"	32	5⅛	123	2⅜	217	2299	623	3139	8	
1/56	9108	DOME	YES	19'3"	32	5⅛	123	2⅜	217	2299	623	3139	9	

A   The engine was identical with 6203. Tender fitted was 9130 of 9 tons, standard 4000 gallons capacity.

B   Tender 9130 replaced by tender 9361 of 10 ton capacity.

Speedos, AWS

Amongst the last modifications to LMS and most of the bigger BR engines in fact, was the belated provision of speedometers and AWS. The story is much the same as the one outlined in the *Book of the Coronation Pacifics* and *The Book of the Royal Scots*; efforts at 'speed indication' were brought up short by the War and eventually abandoned and when eventually BR fitted suitable equipment from 1957 it had few years of useful life before the engines were withdrawn. Done under works order E7461, the fixing dates (period ending) of the speedos are as follows:

46200	30/11/57
46201	5/10/57
46202*	-
46203	7/9/57
46204 **	-
46205	2/11/57
46206	5/10/57
46207	30/11/57
46208	2/11/57
46209	28/12/57
46210	5/10/57
46211	2/11/57
46212	5/10/57

*46202 destroyed before this.
**46204 – no mention on cards – presumably clerical error (beware!) because photographs show it clearly running with the BR speedo by early 1958.*

The Automatic Warning System – AWS – appeared from 1959, its presence denoted by the protection plate under the buffer beam, below the screw coupling at the front, and the two cylinders on the footplate. The timing reservoir was placed on the left-hand side in front of the cab and the bigger vacuum reservoir on the right-hand side, by the rearmost splasher. The battery box was also on the right-hand side, in what was the fairly customary place, close in front of the cab. Dates given for AWS installation seem not to coincide with an obvious visit to Crewe, though it was definitely a works, not a shed job. Take 46200 for instance. She got AWS (then called ATC – Automatic Train Control, under Order E4983) period ending 11/7/59; she was in Crewe for 43 days 29/4/59 to 18/6/59 for 'LC(EO)', that is, Light Casual (Engine Order) and this period is surely the one which saw the AWS fitted – the 'period would have been four weeks. Dates are as follows:

46200	11/7/59
46201	no details
46202	-
46203	13/6/59
46204	13/6/59
46205	28/11/59

46207 PRINCESS ARTHUR (how we puzzled at that name) OF CONNAUGHT with the up Shamrock at Tring. Photograph J. Robertson, B.P. Hoper Collection.

ENGINE 46210 LADY PATRICIA

DATE	DETAILS OF BOILERS FITTED				Large Tubes		Small Tubes		HEATING SURFACE (SQ FT)				PHASE (SEE NOTES)	
	No.	Position of regulator	Comb. Chamber Fitted or not	Length Between Tube Plates	No.	Outs dia (ins)	No.	Outs dia (ins)	Fire-Box	Tubes	Element	Total		
9/35	9108	HEADER	YES	19'3"	32	5⅛	112	2⅜	217	2167	623	3007	3	A
9/36	-	-	-	-	-	-	-	-	-	-	-	-	-	B
4/38	9108	HEADER	YES	19'3"	32	5⅛	112	2⅜	217	2167	623	3007	3	
11/40	9105	HEADER	YES	19'3"	32	5⅛	112	2⅜	217	2167	623	3007	3	
9/43	9236	DOME	YES	19'3"	40	5⅛	81	2¼	217	1951	832	3000	7	
8/44	9106	HEADER	YES	19'3"	32	5⅛	112	2⅜	217	2167	623	3007	3	
7/47	9101	HEADER	YES	19'3"	32	5⅛	123	2⅜	217	2299	623	3139	8	
4/50	9103	HEADER	YES	19'3"	32	5⅛	123	2⅜	217	2299	623	3139	8	
1/53	9107	DOME	YES	19'3"	32	5⅛	123	2⅜	217	2299	623	3139	9	
11/55	6048	DOME	NO	20'9"	32	5⅛	119	2⅜	190	2425	623	3238	6	
1/58	6050	DOME	NO	20'9"	32	5⅛	110	2⅜	190	2310	623	3123	11	C

A   The engine was identical with 6203. The tender fitted was 9131 of 9 ton, 4000 gallon standard design.
B   Tender 9131 replaced by tender 9360 of 10 ton capacity.
C   The engine was fitted with steam operated cylinder cocks.

ENGINE 46211 QUEEN MAUD

DATE	DETAILS OF BOILERS FITTED				Large Tubes		Small Tubes		HEATING SURFACE (SQ FT)				PHASE (SEE NOTES)	
	No.	Position of regulator	Comb. Chamber Fitted or not	Length Between Tube Plates	No.	Outs dia (ins)	No.	Outs dia (ins)	Fire-Box	Tubes	Element	Total		
9/35	9109	HEADER	YES	19'3"	32	5⅛	112	2⅜	217	2167	623	3007	3	A
6/36	-	-	-	-	-	-	-	-	-	-	-	-	-	B
2/38	9102	HEADER	YES	19'3"	24	5⅛	141	2⅜	217	2308	467	2992	4	
11/39	9107	HEADER	YES	19'3"	32	5⅛	112	2⅜	217	2167	623	3007	3	
7/42	9102	HEADER	YES	19'3"	24	5⅛	141	2⅜	217	2308	467	2992	4	
5/44	9101	HEADER	YES	19'3"	32	5⅛	123	2⅜	217	2299	623	3139	8	
1/47	9103	HEADER	YES	19'3"	32	5⅛	123	2⅜	217	2299	623	3139	8	
5/49	9100	HEADER	YES	19'3"	32	5⅛	112	2⅜	217	2167	623	3007	3	
11/52	9235	DOME	YES	19'3"	32	5⅛	123	2⅜	217	2299	623	3139	9	
1/56	9102	DOME	YES	19'3"	32	5⅛	123	2⅜	217	2299	623	3139	9	
7/58	6048	DOME	NO	20'9"	32	5⅛	119	2⅜	190	2425	623	3238	6	C

A   The engine was identical with 6203. The tender fitted was 9132 of 9 tons, 4000 gallons standard design.
B   Tender 9132 was replaced by tender 9345 of 10 ton capacity.
C   The engine was fitted with steam operated cylinder cocks.

If it was one train the Lizzies can be forever associated with, it would surely be The Merseyside Express. 46208 PRINCESS HELENA VICTORIA takes its turn on the down train south of Watford, in the middle 1950s; it went to Edge Hill at the beginning of that decade and seems to have stayed there to the end. With a train signalled on the up main, pity the poor photographer...

ENGINE 46212 DUCHESS OF KENT

DATE	DETAILS OF BOILERS FITTED				Large Tubes		Small Tubes		HEATING SURFACE (SQ FT)				PHASE (SEE NOTES)	
	No.	Position of regulator	Comb. Chamber Fitted or not	Length Between Tube Plates	No.	Outs dia (ins)	No.	Outs dia (ins)	Fire-box	Tubes	Element	Total		
10/35	9235	DOME	YES	19'3"	32	5⅛	112	2⅜	217	2167	623	3007	5	A
7/36	-	-	-	-	-	-	-	-	-	-	-	-	-	B
5/37	9107	HEADER	YES	19'3"	32	5⅛	112	2⅜	217	2167	623	3007	3	
7/39	9235	DOME	YES	19'3"	32	5⅛	112	2⅜	217	2167	623	3007	5	
6/43	9100	HEADER	YES	19'3"	32	5⅛	112	2⅜	217	2167	623	3007	3	
12/45	9105	HEADER	YES	19'3"	32	5⅛	112	2⅜	217	2167	623	3007	3	
3/49	9107	HEADER	YES	19'3"	32	5⅛	123	2⅜	217	2299	623	3139	8	
10/52	6049	DOME	NO	20'9"	32	5⅛	119	2⅜	190	2425	623	3238	6	
1/54	9236	DOME	YES	19'3"	40	5⅛	101	2⅜	217	2232	720	3169	10	

A   The engine was identical with 6203. The tender fitted was 9133 of 9 ton, 4000 gallons standard design.

B   Tender 9133 replaced by tender 9354 of 10 ton capacity.

46206	18/4/59
46207	21/3/59
46208	3/10/59
46209	13/6/59
46210	-
46211	21/3/59
46212	13/6/59

46203 and 46210 were in Scotland and the equipment was not planned for the routes they were used on. They were scrapped without getting AWS.

LIVERIES

Livery variations are the spawn of the devil though the story so far as the Princess Royals are concerned is not as bad as it might be. A summary follows, right:

LIVERY CHANGES

No	First Liv.	LMS black	BRblack	BRblue	BRgreen	BRred
6200	Red	9/47	-	-	4/52	5/58+
6201	Red	8/47	2/48	-	4/52	-
6202	Red	5/47	3/49	-	8/52	-
6203	Red	12/47	-	5/51	3/52	-
6204	Red	-	-	-	5/52	8/58#
6205	Red	-	11/48*	-	9/52	-
6206	Red	2/48	-	11/50	8/53*	-
6207	Red	-	5/49	-	12/51	5/58+
6208	Red	-	-	9/50	11/52	9/58#
6209	Red	-	5/48	-	9/51	-
6210	Red	8/47	-	5/50*	3/53*	-
6211	Red	2/47	6/49*	-	12/52*	-
6212	Red	-	4/49	-	11/52*	-

*approximate—probably into service some weeks later
+LMS style lining
#BR style lining

It's all in that front end... 46210 LADY PATRICIA at Shrewsbury shed after a filling in turn, about 1956. Photograph B.P. Hoper Collection.

46212 DUCHESS OF KENT in BR black, warming up at Polmadie for the night's work ahead, 3 June 1950. Photograph J.L. Stevenson.

From new, then, the Princess Royals carried red, or 'crimson lake' if you prefer, adorned with 12in. gold characters, black shaded.

From 1936 some (three or four) got the rather utilitarian 'sans serif' lettering.

From 1938 came yellow (or even in some cases gold – possibly) characters with red shading. In black and white photographs the differences are hardly clear cut.

In 1946 the stylish LMS '1946 black' with red and straw lining and art deco block numbers made its appearance. In 1948-49 some, particularly those not yet in LMS black, got the BR lined 'LNWR' black. BRITISH RAILWAYS appears on tenders with new numbers. Four become blue in 1950-51, including 46203, which carried the new garb for only six months. It was ex-works on 24/5/51 but was in service thus only until 13/11 the same year, when it went to Derby, of all places. It didn't emerge from there until 17/3/52, in Brunswick green. It was therefore in blue for no more than six months.

From 1951 it's BR Brunswick green with first emblem; the second emblem comes in during 1957 and in the following year four of them get 'BR red'. Of these four, 46200 and 46207 were turned out in a style that closely followed their original LMS livery. The lining was therefore black and yellow and the cabside lining was to the edge of the cab and extended vertically to the cab roof. 46204 and 46208 on the other hand, though they too were turned out in red, had BR lining, namely black and orange, and the cabside lining was limited to a rectangular panel below the window

which was 'set in' from the edge. Both of these locos were later modified to LMS style lining, so all four 1950s 'red' Princesses ended up looking the same.

A note on emblems is also useful; here it is as explained (courtesy again Mr. Eric Youldon) in *The Book of the Royal Scots*: The first Emblem, introduced mid-1949, had right-hand and left-hand versions so that whichever side the loco was viewed, the lion faced 'forwards', towards the loco. The second Emblem, generally introduced in March 1957, first appeared as a 'preview' on 70016 in 1956. It followed the 1949 one, being initially produced in right-hand and left-hand versions. However, this drew the displeasure of the College of Heralds, insofar as the right-hand one was concerned, so only the left-hand one was permitted. The change was effected from September 1958 and from then on only the left-facing lion was applied, which meant that on the right-hand side of the engine the lion faced towards the rear.

Names
The first Pacific, 6200, did

its first work without a name, though it appeared within weeks, firstly as simply PRINCESS ROYAL. 6201 also ran for a while without a name and apparently did not get its plates until mid-December 1933. The later batch of ten entered traffic named, and the reconstituted Turbomotive was named on Princess Anne's birthday, 15 August 1952. Apparently *The Railway Observer* expected that the names of the original Pacifics, 6200-6202, would be Greek heroes, AGAMEMNON, ACHILLES and so on but this seems simply to have been a rumour. Some minor correspondence in *The Railway Gazette* elicited this official explanation from the LMS, see below:

46203 PRINCESS MARGARET ROSE

Built Crewe
LM 'date built' 1 July 1935
Renumbered 6203 to 46203 week ending 22/5/48

REPAIRS	
All Crewe unless	18/9/47-8/12/47**HG** (71)
stated otherwise	26/2/48-5/5/48**HO** (59)
Figure in brackets	16/11/48-23/12/48**LS** (33)
= weekdays out of traffic	18/2/49-13/5/49**HC** (72)
19/6/36-6/4/36**LS**	5/8/49-15/9/49**LC** (36)
8/4/36-15/4/36**LO**	16/10/49-28/10/49**NC** (11)
15/6/36-19/6/36**LO**	3/6/50-3/7/50**LI** (26)
6/8/36-17/8/36**HO**	17/4/51-24/5/51**HG** (32)
30/11/36-19/1/37**HG** (43)	13/11/51-17/3/52**HI** (105)*Derby*
5/8/37-10/9/37**HS** (32)	4/4/52-4/4/52**NC(EO)** (1)
29/11/37-13/12/37**LO** (13)	8/4/52-10/4/52**NC(Rect)EO** (2)
12/11/38-12/2/39**HG** (67)	29/4/53-15/5/53**LC** (14)
28/12/39-13/1/40**LS** (15)	20/8/53-24/9/53**HC** (30)
24/940-12/10/40**LO**(17)	29/10/53-4/12/53**HI** (31)
25/1/41-22/2/41**HC**(25)	22/2/54-19/3/54**HC(EO)** (22)
15/11/41-20/12/41**HG**	8/9/54-16/10/54**HC(EO)** (33)
20/3/42-16/4/42**LO**	19/8/55-19/10/55**HG** (52)
13/11/42-15/12/42**HS**	29/10/55-10/11/55**NC(Rect)EO** (10)
27/7/43-18/8/43**HS** (20)	10/2/56-13/3/56**LC(EO)** (29)
21/9/43-30/9/43**LO** (9)	28/10/56-21/12/56**HI** (46)
11/6/44-26/9/44**HG** (39)	1/6/57-3/8/57**LC(EO)** (54)
28/5/45-30/6/45**HS** (36)	23/9/57-26/9/57**NC(EO)** (3)
26/10/45-16/11/45**LO** (19)	18/10/57-7/12/57**LC(EO)** (43)
24/12/45-9/2/46**HO** (41)	13/6/58-14/8/58**HG** (53)
29/7/46-7/9/46**LS** (36)	13/4/59-22/5/59**LC** (34)
18/1/47-19/8/47**LO** (28)	9/9/59-6/11/59**HI** (50)
28/2/47-20/3/47**LO** (24)	14/6/60-12/8/60**HC(EO)** (51)
	29/11/60-9/2/61**HI** (60)

MILEAGES	
1935	48,585
1936	95,476
1937	74,941
1938	74,017
1939	83,612
1940	57,999
1941	40,375
1942	58,887
1943	57,016
1944	51,086
1945	54,674
1946	67,434
1947	45,690
1948	43,695
1949	44,991
1950	57,921
1951	54,428
1952	59,619
1953	53,119
1954	57,967
1955	51,678
1956	54,457
1957	47,713
1958	56,192
1959	51,431
1960	45,469
1961	6,019
1962	-

Mileage at 31/12/50 956,399
Mileage at 12/61 1,494,491
Withdrawn week ending 20/10/62
Preserved – 'Sold to Messrs. Butlin's Ltd April 1963'.

SHEDS	
Camden	6/7/35
Polmadie	24/8/35
Camden	29/2/36
Edge Hill	21/10/39
Holyhead	6/4/40
Crewe North	28/9/40
Holyhead	2/11/40
Edge Hill	9/11/40
Camden	26/12/42
Edge Hill	3/4/43
Crewe North (loan)	9/10/43
Crewe North	27/11/43
Edge Hill	20/5/44
Crewe North (loan)	18/10/47
Edge Hill	14/2/48
Polmadie	22/9/51
Edge Hill	16/5/53
Crewe North	23/5/53
Edge Hill	20/9/58
Camden	20/8/60
Edge Hill	10/9/60
Carnforth	11/3/61
Crewe North	18/7/61
Carnforth	9/9/61
Carlisle Upperby	27/1/62
Carlisle Kingmoor	7/4/62

TENDERS	
No	Fitted
9124	1/7/35
9374	19/1/37

Now in BR Brunswick green, 46203 runs near to Shap Summit cuttings with the 11.15am down Birmingham New Street to Glasgow Central express on 6 June 1952. It was doing about twenty miles an hour with twelve or thirteen coaches unaided, so the 'specification' for Stanier's Pacifics back in 1932 still held. Photograph E.D. Bruton.

More moorland. PRINCESS MARGARET ROSE lifts the 11.15am down Birmingham New Street to Glasgow Central express (locally termed the 'Birmingham-Scottish') up the 1 in 75 of Shap, near Scout Green, on 26 May 1952. Photograph E.D. Bruton.

46203 blasting out of Edinburgh Princes Street (with an ordinary passenger train – and probably a fill in turn) on 4 April 1953. The Lizzies were not often seen at the Caledonian terminus here – it is slightly surprising that 46203 does not bear one of the Caley 'semaphore' route indicators. Photograph J. Robertson, B.P. Hoper Collection.

46203 PRINCESS MARGARET ROSE passes a local Crab at Carstairs on 17 June 1954. Photograph J. Robertson, B.P. Hoper Collection.

PRINCESS MARGARET ROSE in the shed yard at Carnforth late in 1962, showing that fine high-swept tender to good effect. The shame is that the engine, if not already withdrawn, is only days away from that fate. Photograph B.P. Hoper Collection.

46204 PRINCESS LOUISE

Built Crewe
LM 'date built' 19 July 1935
Renumbered 6204 to 46204 week ending 24/4/48

REPAIRS	
All Crewe unless	24/3/49-4/4/9**NC** (10)
stated otherwise	11/5/49-2/6/49**LC** (18)
Figure in brackets	27/6/49-28/9/49**LC** (81)
= weekdays out of traffic	22/10/49-9/11/49**LC** (16)
	15/4/50-13/9/50**HI** (129)
23/12/35-24/12/35**LO** (2)	15/3/51-17/4/51**LC** (27)
17/4/36-6/5/36**LS** (17)	23/4/51-2/5/51**NC(Rect)** (8)
8/6/36-17/6/36**LO** (9)	19/6/51-4/8/51**LI** (40)
7/8/36-21/8/36**LO** (13)	8/8/51-23/8/51**NC(Rect)(EO)** (13)
11/12/36-19/12/36**LO** (8)	11/9/51-16/10/51**LC(EO)** (30)
28/9/37-15/11/37**HG** (42)	1/11/51-15/12/51**LC(EO)** (38)
21/6/38-3/8/38**HS** (38)	12/1/52-2/2/52**LC** (18)
6/12/38-22/12/38**LO** (15)	28/2/52-26/6/52**HG** (101)
15/8/39-6/9/39**LS** (20)	9/1/53-13/2/53**HC(EO)** (30)
2/9/40-9/10/40**HG** (33)	24/12/53-23/1/54**HI** (24)
9/10/41-31/10/41**LS** (20)	13/9/54-8/11/54**HC(EO)** (48)
2/7/42-5/8/42**HO** (30)	29/3/55-16/4/55**LC(EO)** (15)
8/4/43-1/5/43**HS** (21)	20/5/55-7/7/55**HG** (41)
20/11/43-22/12/43**LO** (28)	3/10/55-27/10/55**LC(EO)** (21)
13/5/44-10/6/44**HG** (25)	17/11/55-23/12/55**HC(EO)** (31)
31/1/45-9/3/45**LS** (33)	28/12/55-19/1/56**LC(EO)** (19)
27/5/45-16/6/45**LO** (17)	25/2/56-19/4/56**LC(EO)** (45)
22/11/45-5/1/46**LS** (38)	4/6/56-26/6/56**NC(Rect)(EO)** (19)
5/9/46-11/10/46**HG** (32)	28/1/57-2/3/57**HI** (29)
27/1/47-15/4/47**HO** (67)	21/8/57-10/10/57**LC(EO)** (43)
2/9/47-15/10/47**HS** (38)	4/7/58-29/8/58**LI** (48)
18/10/47-17/11/47**NC(Rect)** (26)	15/11/58-10/1/59**HC(EO)** (46)
20/11/47-11/12/47**LO** (19)	29/4/59-12/6/59**LC(EO)** (38)
9/3/48-21/4/48**LO** (37)	29/9/59-27/11/59**LI** (51)
3/5/48-20/5/48**NC** (16)	24/3/60-17/5/60**LC(EO)** (45)
30/12/48-10/3/49**LI** (61)	2/12/60-19/11/60**HC(EO)** (41)

SHEDS
Camden 20/7/35
Polmadie 24/12/35
Camden 29/2/36
Crewe North 16/9/39
Edge Hill 21/10/39
Holyhead 6/4/40
Edge Hill 9/11/40
Camden (loan) 21/3/42
Edge Hill 16/5/42
Camden (loan) 17/10/42
Crewe North 22/5/43
Edge Hill 20/5/44
Crewe North 24/5/45
Edge Hill 11/12/48
Crewe North 28/5/49
Edge Hill 1/10/49
Crewe North 10/6/50
Edge Hill 30/9/50
Crewe North 22/6/57
Edge Hill 21/9/57
Crewe North 14/6/58
Edge Hill 5/7/58

TENDERS
No	Fitted
9125	19/7/35
9375	19/12/36

MILEAGES
Year	Miles
1937	70,185
1938	77,070
1939	64,951
1940	57,205
1941	54,749
1942	72,920
1943	53,700
1944	72,767
1945	47,616
1946	61,768
1947	36,395
1948	53,302
1949	30,548
1950	39,581
1951	26,618
1952	48,904
1953	64,799
1954	51,575
1955	49,064
1956	44,968
1957	48,044
1958	44,974
1959	38,644
1960	34,845
1961	11,370

Mileage at 31/12/50 910,140
Mileage at 10/61 1,373,945
Withdrawn week ending 7/10/61
Scrapped Crewe Works 5/62

Below. PRINCESS LOUISE, a Princess Royal resplendent in full crimson lake ('red' just doesn't seem the same) at Shrewsbury in the old days. That spindly pipe leading to the rear driving wheel crank pin can only be one of the early speed indicator fitments; it would be one of the Hasler pattern fitted from 1936 and abandoned a year or so later as unreliable. The loco also has steam sanding. The picture shows well the more compact slidebars of the production 'run'. Vacuum pump already removed but drive arm bracket still in position on crosshead.

PRINCESS LOUISE with the up Shamrock, coming over the
flyover having just left Primrose Hill Tunnel, in July 1954.
The Slow lines run below with DC lines leaving to 're-join'
later. Behind is Camden No.2 signal box.

46204 blurs slightly through the telegraph wires on Sunday 14 September 1958, west of Milford & Brockton station, on the way to Stafford. PRINCESS LOUISE is in BR style red ('maroon') livery, newly acquired only a few weeks before; the train is the 2.20pm Euston to Liverpool Lime Street. Shows speedo drive to good effect. Photograph Michael Mensing.

In scruffy condition, 46204 PRINCESS LOUISE makes it way along Trent Valley line near Rugby, with the Merseyside Express, 20 June 1958. This was a matter of weeks before its works visit of 4/7/58-29/8/58, which saw it emerge in BR red 'maroon'. Photograph B.P. Hoper Collection.

Rugby Midland station, and 46204 stands in the bay platform at the north end, picking up vans for a down working. The date is not known, but it is late in the day; overhead wires are in place (but not live) and the engine has speedo and AWS. Photograph B.P. Hoper Collection.

The chimneys of the 1935 batch of ten had more 'curve' to them than the original two engines, with much less – possibly nothing – of a parallel between top and bottom. The difference is plain to see in some views, much less so in others. The 'new' curve stands out well against a background of steam as PRINCESS LOUISE waits at Carlisle station, 11 March 1961. Photograph B.P. Hoper Collection.

46205 PRINCESS VICTORIA

Built Crewe
LM 'date built' 24 July 1935
Renumbered 6205 to 46205 week ending 22/5/48

REPAIRS
All Crewe unless
stated otherwise
Figure in brackets
= weekdays out of traffic
15/5/36-29/5/36**LS** (13)
18/6/36-25/6/36**LO** (7)
1/7/36-17/7/36**LO** (15)
9/11/36-25/11/36**LO** (15)
22/3/37-20/4/37**HS** (25)
3/2/38-11/5/38**HG** (83)
7/9/38-26/9/38**LO** (17)
28/1/39-20/2/39**LS** (20)
20/10/39-29/11/39**TRO** (35)
13/3/40-17/4/40**LO** (30)
1/1/41 -14/2/41**HG** (39)
24/2/41-13/3/41**LO** (16)
31/1/42-24/2/42**HS** (21)
3/10/42-25/11/42**HG** (46)
19/2/43-26/2/43**LO** (7)
15/10/43-23/10/43**LO** (8)
21/2/44-11/3/44**LS** (18)
11/8/44-23/9/44**LO** (44)
24/1/45-17/2/45**HG** (22)
24/8/45-8/11/45**LO** (66)
18/3/46-10/4/46**HS** (21)
12/6/46-17/7/46**LO** (31)
8/11/46-7/12/46**HO** (26)
5/5/47-19/6/47**LO** (40)

7/9/47-31/10/47**LS** (47)
16/12/47-11/2/48**HO** (49)
17/6/48-31/7/48**LO** (39)
24/9/48-5/11/48**HG** (37)
11/2/49-17/3/49**HC** (30)
5/10/49-4/11/49**LI** (27)
12/5/50-9/6/50**LC** (24)
28/12/50-26/1/51**LI** (25)
6/2/51-15/3/51**HC** (32)
19/3/51-28/3/51**NC** (7)
23/8/51-19/10/51**LC(EO)** (49)
19/11/51-4/1/52**LC** (38)
6/5/52-9/9/52**HG** (108)
4/2/54-3/4/54**HI** (50)
8/4/54-9/4/54**NC(Rect)(EO)** (1)
8/6/54-4/8/54**LC(EO)** (49)
13/12/54-27/1/55**LC(EO)** (37)
9/11/55-4/2/56**HG** (73)
16/5/56-23/6/56**LC** (33)
20/3/57-4/5/57**HI** (38)
7/5/57-10/5/57**NC(Rect)(EO)** (3)
28/10/57-31/10/57**NC(EO)** (3)
23/12/57-13/2/58**LC(EO)** (43)
14/8/58-2/10/58**HG** (42)
10/10/59-11/11/59**NC(EO)** (27)
30/4/60-26/2/60**LI** (50)
13/4/60-21/5/60**LC(EO)** (32)
16/8/60-4/10/60**LC(EO)** (42)

SHEDS
Camden 27/7/35
Polmadie 3/8/35
Camden 28/9/35
Edge Hill 21/10/39
Polmadie (loan) 9/12/39
Edge Hill 30/1/40
Holyhead 16/4/40
Crewe North 2/11/40
Edge Hill 20/1/44
Carlisle Upperby (loan) 12/7/47
Crewe North (loan) 18/10/47
Edge Hill 21/2/48
Crewe North 21/12/48
Edge Hill 1/10/49
Crewe North 7/7/51
Edge Hill 15/9/51
Crewe North 10/11/51
Edge Hill 20/9/52
Crewe North 22/6/57
Willesden 11/3/61
Camden 15/7/61
Willesden 9/9/61

TENDERS

No	Fitted
9126	24/7/35
9344	29/5/36
9353	17/7/36
9344	11/3/37

MILEAGES

1937	85,168
1938	67,657
1939	67,174
1940	44,395
1941	57,343
1942	49,048
1943	65,184
1944	64,346
1945	57,332
1946	44,659
1947	43,125
1948	41,872
1949	62,096
1950	51,015
1951	33,793
1952	49,913
1953	65,044
1954	45,868
1955	49,546
1956	53,971
1957	61,095
1958	53,212
1959	65,888
1960	27,108
1961	20,459

Mileage at 31/12/50 920,691
Mileage at 11/61 1,446,588
Withdrawn week ending 25/11/61
Scrapped Crewe Works 5/62

6205 juts out majestically from the tumble-down shed at Carlisle Upperby; the date is unfortunately unrecorded but it would be about 1947. The high building behind was the Upperby Repair Shop, once one of the LNWR major 'outstation shops' but long out of use for that purpose. The roofless shed building was replaced by the familiar concrete roundhouse early on in BR days. Photograph W. Hermiston, B.P. Hoper Collection.

Polmadie, and Crewe North's Lizzie, 46205 PRINCESS VICTORIA in BR (LNW) lined black stands resplendent and ready for the next Mid-Day Scot back to London. It looks to be a typically breezy Glasgow day – look at how those minor steam leaks are blowing back! This is the perfect view to illustrate 46205's odd valve gear, the cumbersome motion bracket indicating the new valves and motion fitted in March 1938. Rocking levers were provided so that the two inside sets of gear could be removed. The outside motion then also worked the valve gear of the inside cylinders. PRINCESS VICTORIA remained the only Princess Royal to be so treated. Photograph J. Robertson, B.P. Hoper Collection.

Transfer to Crewe North took 46205 off the Liverpool-London trains and on to longer workings. Here it is on the down Mid-Day Scot, passing through Tamworth on 8 March 1958. Photograph Michael Mensing.

46205 PRINCESS VICTORIA in its last year, at Rugby heading north, perhaps on the through line. The distant girdering above and beyond the train is the Great Central overbridge and just about discernible on it is the blurred but unmistakable outline of a southbound 9F 2-10-0. Photograph B.P. Hoper Collection.

46206 PRINCESS MARIE LOUISE

Built Crewe
LM 'date built' 1 August 1935
Renumbered 6206 to 46206 week ending 27/11/48

REPAIRS

All Crewe unless
stated otherwise
Figure in brackets
= weekdays out of traffic
18/11/35-24/12/35**LO** (32)
23/7/36-31/7/36**LO** (8)
21/9/36-15/10/36**LS** (22)
12/3/37-24/3/37**LO** (11)
22/6/37-13/8/37**HG** (46)
18/8/38-14/9/38**HS** (24)
20/6/39-29/7/39**HG** (35)
2/2/40-17/2/40**LO** (14)
19/8/40-21/9/40**HS** (30)
24/4/41-15/5/41**LS** (19)
12/12/41-10/1/42**LS** (25)
25/3/42-16/4/42**LO** (20)
13/10/42-9/1/43**HG** (74)
18/3/43-15/4/43**LO** (25)
5/8/43-2/9/43**HO** (25)
8/12/43-13/1/44**LO** (31)
12/4/44-9/5/44**LS** (24)
10/7/44-29/7/44**LO** (18)
16/12/44-13/1/45**LO** (24)

6/7/45-7/8/45**HG** (28)
8/11/45-1/12/45**LO** (21)
6/8/46-16/9/46**LS** (36)
13/11/46-3/1/47**HO** (44)
14/5/47-30/6/47**LO** (41)
7/11/47-15/11/47**NC** (41)
11/12/47-4/3/48**HG** (72)
15/10/48-24/11/48**HS** (35)
27/11/50-2/12/50**NC (Rect)** (5)
6/12/50-19/12/50**NC(Rect)** (11)
29/3/52-3/5/52**LI** (29)
7/5/52-16/5/52**NC(Rect)** (8)
2/9/52-3/10/52**HC(EO)** (27)
24/2/53-27/3/53**LC(EO)** (27)
30/5/53-4/8/53**HI** (56)
11/2/55-2/4/55**HG** (43)
29/9/56-10/11/56**LI** (36)
19/9/57-21/9/57**NC(EO)** (2)
21/1/58-7/3/58**HG** (39)
4/2/59-4/4/59**HI** (50)
3/3/60-30/4/60**LI** (49)
6/7/60-18/8/60**HC(EO)** (37)
3/11/60-5/1/61**LC(EO)** (52)

TENDERS

No	Fitted
9127	1/8/35
9359	15/10/36
9353	20/11/46
9359	17/10/47
9816	18/10/62

This last 'transfer' was the welded Duchess tender, which may well have been a 'paper' exercise only.

SHEDS

Crewe North 10/8/35
Camden 24/8/35
Longsight 15/7/39
Edge Hill 2/12/39
Camden 6/4/40
Crewe North 2/6/42
Camden 22/5/43
Crewe North 16/10/43
Camden (loan) 23/6/51
Crewe North 21/7/51
Edge Hill 25/9/54
Crewe North 23/10/54
Rugby 11/3/61
Crewe North 8/7/61
Rugby 9/9/61
Camden 27/1/62

MILEAGES

1935	30,178
1936	86,001
1937	83,805
1938	74,968
1939	62,403
1940	62,837
1941	75,867
1942	48,453
1943	60,403
1944	40,462
1945	51,880
1946	47,491
1947	44,536
1948	47,981
1949	53,755
1950	31,030
1951	75,729
1952	69,582
1953	56,302
1954	61,512
1955	56,401
1956	55,297
1957	76,408
1958	59,988
1959	64,184
1960	39,054
1961	17,039
1962	18,587

Mileage at 31/12/50 902,050
Mileage at 11/62 1,533,546, if calculated; the Record Card gives a 'Life Mileage' of 1,552,133
Withdrawn week ending 3/11/62
Scrapped Crewe Works 10/62

Hastily incorporated in to the BR scheme of things with 'M6206' at the front and 6206 with 'M' underneath on its cabside, Crewe North's PRINCESS MARIE LOUISE runs past Berkhamsted and its mailbag pick-up, 15 May 1948. Photograph H.C. Casserley.

PRINCESS MARIE LOUISE, renumbered in the first BR style after the crude 'M' addition, at Polmadie on 2 July 1950. Photograph J.L. Stevenson.

46206 PRINCESS MARIE LOUISE on the down Mid-Day Scot at Standish Junction in August 1957. Photograph B.P. Hoper Collection.

Two curious pictures of 46206 still, it seems, in blue. The year is thought to be 1953, and the place Shrewsbury. 46206 has worked in hard from somewhere, to judge from the coal but it is now engaged on the thoroughly unfamiliar task of shunting a five plank wagon! There is also a good view of the only Princess Royal 'coal pusher' tender, with steam pipes and lubricating valves at the back laid out just like the tenders of the 'big 'uns' – the Coronation Pacifics. Because the Coronation tenders were welded, it was the only coal pusher tender that was riveted. Other Lizzies could haul the tender (No.9359), but only 46206, with the necessary steam connections, could operate it. Both photographs B.P. Hoper Collection.

46206 PRINCESS MARIE LOUISE, in blue livery, leaves Rugby for the north with the Mid-Day Scot.

PRINCESS MARIE LOUISE with a train at Carlisle, 23 August 1952. This seems to be just north of the station – it's just possible to make out the goods lines at a slightly lower level through the bridge. Photograph J. Robertson, B.P. Hoper Collection.

46207 PRINCESS ARTHUR OF CONNAUGHT

Built Crewe
LM 'date built' 9 August 1935
Renumbered 6207 to 46207 week ending 14/5/49

REPAIRS

All Crewe unless
stated otherwise
Figure in brackets
= weekdays out of traffic

9/12/35-13/1/36**LO** (30)	5/9/49-10/10/49**LC** (31)
9/4/36-8/5/36**LO** (25)	17/4/50-20/5/50**HI** (29)
15/6/36-24/6/36**LO** (9)	25/12/50-18/1/51**NC** (20)
1/10/36-28/10/36**HS** (24)	20/1/51-24/1/51**NC** (3)
23/8/37-6/10/37**HG** (39)	31/1/51-1/3/51**LC** (25)
2/7/38-8/8/38**HS** (32)	21/6/51-23/6/51**NC** (6)
14/2/39-21/3/39**LO** (31)	23/9/51-22/12/51**HG** (77)
22/5/39-14/6/39**LO** (21)	*Weedon-see 'How To Rescue*
1/1/40-3/2/40**HG** (30)	*A Princess'*
20/2/40-9/3/40**LO** (17)	26/9/52-31/10/52**LC(EO)** (30)
30/9/40-19/10/40**LO** (18)	6/11/52-7/11/52**NC (Rect) EO** (1)
6/3/41-29/3/41**LS** (21)	8/1/53-16/2/53**HI** (33)
19/11/41-24/1/42**HG** (57)	9/11/53-1/1/54**HI** (44)
27/2/42-23/3/42**LO** (21)	9/3/54-27/3/54**LC(EO)** (16)
10/4/43-8/6/43**LG** (24)	11/12/54-25/1/55**HI** (36)
6/11/43-31/12/43**HS** (47)	21/4/55-18/5/55**LC** (23)
27/10/44-2/12/44**LO** (32)	26/10/55-9/12/55**HG** (38)
27/6/45-13/9/45**LS** (68)	20/8/56-10/9/56**LC(EO)** (18)
17/5/46-17/6/46**HG** (27)	29/3/57-15/5/37**LI** (39)
2/10/47-14/11/47**HS** (38)	25/6/57-9/7/57**NC(EO)** (12)
19/11/47-2/12/47**NC (Rect)** (12)	2/11/57-9/11/57**NC(EO)** (6)
26/2/48-30/3/48**LO** (28)	8/3/58-9/5/58**HG** (52)
24/11/48-10/5/49**HG** (142)	24/9/58-24/10/58**LC(EO)** (26)
19/5/49-28/5/49**LC** (9)	17/11/58-5/12/58**LC(EO)** (16)
	17/1/59-14/3/59**LC(EO)** (48)
	14/5/59-8/7/59**LI** (47)
	29/10/60-3/12/60**HI** (30)
	12/1/61-11/2/61**LC(EO)** (26)

MILEAGES

Year	Miles
1935	30,038
1936	94,863
1937	83,354
1938	89,055
1939	58,397
1940	60,387
1941	59,636
1942	50,929
1943	40,059
1944	41,485
1945	59,692
1946	72,008
1947	41,543
1948	55,920
1949	37,026
1950	62,328
1951	40,078
1952	63,101
1953	56,864
1954	61,176
1955	52,304
1956	64,745
1957	56,911
1958	55,406
1959	49,966
1960	50,086
1961	15,338

Mileage at 31/12/50 936,730
Mileage at 11/61 1,502,705
Withdrawn week ending 25/11/61
Scrapped Crewe Works 5/62

SHEDS

Crewe North 10/8/35
Camden 31/8/35
Crewe North 4/8/38
Camden 27/8/38
Rugby 16/9/39
Longsight 21/10/39
Camden 2/12/39
Edge Hill 1/6/40
Crewe North 10/8/40
Edge Hill 22/9/51
Western Region 4/2/56
Edge Hill 25/2/56
Camden 3/10/59
Willesden 11/3/61
Camden 15/7/61
Willesden 9/9/61

TENDERS

No	Fitted
9128	9/8/35
9376	18/12/36
9353	25/12/39
9359	20/11/46
9353	17/10/47

Smoothly, glisteningly new, 6207 PRINCESS ARTHUR OF CONNAUGHT (with original 'standard' tender) stands in the shed yard at Crewe North, 18 August 1935, Photograph Locofotos.

The Princess Royals did not have long, once the batch of ten was completed in 1935, to dominate the Anglo-Scottish expresses. Once the Coronations became available in 1937 they were seen less on such 'top' trains, though of course the Lizzies were still ready for jobs such as The Royal Scot when needed. This is 6207 PRINCESS ARTHUR OF CONNAUGHT with the up train, leaving Carlisle on 21 June 1937, the very month the first three Coronations, 6220-6222, went in to traffic. Photograph H.C. Casserley.

6207 PRINCESS ARTHUR OF CONNAUGHT at Polmadie about 1947, shining in a lovely low northern light. Photograph J.L. Stevenson.

PRINCESS ARTHUR OF CONNAUGHT visits Polmadie about 1948; the marks on the boiler show where someone has been attending to the top feed, disrupting the grime in the process and possibly revealing something of the red underneath! Photograph W. Hermiston, B.P. Hoper Collection.

Super power on the 8am ex-Liverpool, at Bletchley on 1 August 1953. Black Five 4-6-0 No.45097 is the leading engine. Note LNER still on coach! Photograph M.N. Bland, B.P. Hoper Collection.

Two further deserved outings for Peter Groom's wonderful two pictures of 46207 PRINCESS ARTHUR OF CONNAUGHT at Euston on The Mid-Day Scot. (They were published in the Irwell Press *Great British Stations – Euston*.) The date was 31 August 1961, and very probably the last occasion on which a Princess Royal was diagrammed to this train; this was in the days of John Fore, ADMPS at Camden and determined to let them have a 'last fling'.

THE RED REVOLUTION. 46207 PRINCESS ARTHUR OF CONNAUGHT after arrival at Euston and later on Camden shed, followed there by the photographer in time-honoured fashion. The livery can only be red – observe the lining on footplate/cylinders, for instance. The date is 19 May 1958, and the BR red had been put on only a fortnight or so before. Photographs J. Robertson, B.P. Hoper Collection.

46208 PRINCESS HELENA VICTORIA

Built Crewe
LM 'date built' 16 August 1935
Renumbered 6208 to 46208 week ending 22/5/48

REPAIRS

All Crewe unless	5/4/46-26/4/46**LO** (18)
stated otherwise	7/9/46-10/10/46**LO** (29)
Figure in brackets	14/1/47-20/2/47**HS** (33)
= weekdays out of traffic	18/8/47-2/9/47**LO** (14)
31/1/36-21/2/36**LO**	10/9/47-24/10/47**LO** (39)
15/6/36-17/6/36**LO**	17/3/48-18/5/48**HG** (53)
29/6/36-3/7/36**LO**	11/9/48-18/10/48**LO** (32)
2/8/36-20/8/36**LS**	11/5/49-21/6/49**LI** (36)
7/3/37-6/5/37**HG** (51)	incomplete -22/9/50**HG**
16/10/37-1/11/37**HO** (14)	14/8/51-19/9/51**HI** (31)
17/11/37-18/12/37**LO** (19)	13/10/51-16/11/51**HC** (29)
18/3/38-2/5/38**HO** (38)	23/7/52-6/11/52**HG** (91)
11/8/38-2/9/38**LS** (20)	20/5/54-18/6/54**LC** (25)
4/6/39-18/7/39**LS** (30)	10/11/54-15/12/54**LI** (30)
28/3/40-3/5/40**HG** (32)	26/10/55-10/12/55**HI** (39)
6/3/41-5/4/41**HS** (27)	21/2/56-20/3/56**LC(EO)** (24)
15/12/41-10/1/42**LS** (23)	4/4/56-28/4/56**NC(Rect)(EO)** (21)
19/1/42-7/2/42**LO** (18)	20/2/57-3/4/57**HG** (36)
26/3/42-25/4/42**LO** (27)	11/4/57-18/4/57**NC(Rect)(EO)** (6)
10/9/42-3/10/42**HO** (21)	18/9/57-22/10/57**LC(EO)** (29)
2/2/43-18/3/43**LO** (39)	20/2/58-2/4/58**LC(EO)** (35)
27/7/43-3/9/43**LS** (34)	13/8/58-24/9/58**LI** (36)
2/11/44-9/12/44**LS** (33)	8/12/58-20/1/59**LC(EO)** (35)
1/1/45-13/1/45**LO** (12)	22/9/59-3/10/59**NC(EO)** (10)
12/7/45-13/10/45**HG** (81)	12/11/59-13/1/60**HG** (51)
5/11/45-1/12/45**LO** (24)	17/5/60-18/5/60**NC(EO)** (1)
6/12/45-27/12/45**LO** (18)	29/5/60-2/9/60**HC(EO)**
14/1/46-2/3/46**LO** (42)	30/10/60-29/12/60**LC(EO)** (73)

SHEDS

Crewe North 18/8/35
Camden 31/8/35
Crewe North (loan) 16/7/38
Camden 6/8/38
Longsight 21/10/39
Camden 2/12/39
Edge Hill 8/6/40
Crewe North 10/8/40
Edge Hill 22/9/51

TENDERS

No	Fitted
9129	16/8/35
9344	3/7/36
9353	11/3/37
9360	16/6/39

MILEAGES

1935	35,330
1936	96,158
1937	66,060
1938	85,613
1939	66,181
1940	68,138
1941	53,996
1942	46,878
1943	54,710
1944	35,058
1945	37,509
1946	56,711
1947	49,233
1948	55,381
1949	60,780
1950	24,746
1951	54,966
1952	49,154
1953	66,601
1954	49,169
1955	58,896
1956	53,110
1957	53,825
1958	47,429
1959	49,777
1960	37,721
1961	15,917
1962	18,634

Mileage at 31/12/50 892,482
Mileage at 10/62 1,449,634
Withdrawn week ending 20/10/62
Scrapped Crewe Works 11/62

6208 PRINCESS HELENA VICTORIA, new at Crewe with lower capacity 'Stanier' tender; vacuum pump drive on the crosshead.

A sparkling new Princess, 6208 PRINCESS HELENA VICTORIA with original tender, on the down Royal Scot at Rugby, about 1935-36. Photograph T.G. Hepburn.

HELENA VICTORIA in traffic at the south end of Crewe, now with high ten ton tender attached, 31 May 1947. Photograph H.C. Casserley.

6208, with Jubilee 5598 BASUTOLAND alongside; the date is unknown, but the 1B Camden plate suggests 1938 or 1939. The livery is red, with what looks like the later, more elegant characters. Photograph W. Hermiston, B.P. Hoper Collection.

What else but The Merseyside Express?(see 'Lizzies from the Lineside' for instance). 46208 hurries it along southwards, near Tring, on 3 August 1956. Photograph J. Robertson, B.P. Hoper Collection.

46209 PRINCESS BEATRICE

Built Crewe
LM 'date built' 23 August 1935
Renumbered 6209 to 46209 week ending 22/1/49

REPAIRS

All Crewe unless	5/2/47-26/3/47**HS** (43)
stated otherwise	1/7/47-5/9/47**LO** (58)
Figure in brackets	9/12/47-9/1/48**HO** (27)
= weekdays out of traffic	16/10/48-18/1/49**HG** (80)
12/12/35-16/1/36**LO**	13/6/49-15/8/49**LC** (55)
14/9/36-1/10/36**LS**	24/11/49-4/1/50**LC** (33)
11/2/37-24/3/37**HG** (36)	17/4/50-25/5/50**LI** (34)
6/1/38-29/1/38**HS** (21)	16/11/50-17/2/51**HC** (79)
15/10/38-21/11/38**HG** (32)	15/8/51-8/10/51**HG** (46)
2/8/39-25/8/39**LS** (21)	21/10/51-9/11/51**NC (Rect) EO** (16)
26/3/40-9/4/40**LO** (13)	20/3/52-25/4/52**LC(EO)** (30)
21/10/40-11/11/40**LS** (15)	17/11/52-24/12/52**LI** (32)
8/2/41-1/3/41**LO** (19)	14/5/53-25/5/53**LC** (9) *shed repair*
21/7/41-16/8/41**HG** (24)	3/12/53-23/1/54**HI** (42)
23/2/42-14/3/42**HS** (18)	26/10/54-3/12/54**LC(EO)** (33)
29/5/42-20/6/42**LO** (20)	28/11/55-18/2/56**HG** (69)
14/12/42-19/1/43**LS** (31)	3/12/56-11/1/57**LC(EO)** (32)
8/3/43-12/4/43**LO** (31)	28/10/57-11/12/57**LI** (38)
27/9/43-4/12/43**HG** (60)	8/10/58-10/12/58**HG** (54)
28/12/44-3/2/45**LS** (33)	4/2/59-22/5/59**LC** (91)
1/10/45-21/12/45**HG** (71)	26/8/59-3/10/59**LC(EO)** (33)
7/8/46-25/10/46**HO** (69)	19/12/60-10/3/61**LI** (44)

SHEDS

Crewe 29/8/35
Camden 7/9/35
Crewe North (loan) 12/2/38
Camden 19/2/38
Longsight 16/9/39
Camden 2/12/39
Crewe North 2/5/42
Edge Hill 6/9/58
Crewe North 20/6/59
Carlisle Upperby 13/8/60
Crewe North 3/9/60
Camden 27/1/62

TENDERS

No	Fitted
9361	1/10/36
9354	4/9/46

MILEAGES

1935	34,662
1936	101,545
1937	78,909
1938	70,978
1939	59,095
1940	71,341
1941	72,988
1942	61,471
1943	50,336
1944	60,617
1945	50,396
1946	53,233
1947	40,690
1948	47,628
1949	53,132
1950	54,737
1951	43,933
1952	65,925
1953	51,410
1954	60,756
1955	63,443
1956	62,743
1957	59,635
1958	49,762
1959	47,100
1960	67,327
1961	14,985
1962	29,218

Mileage at 31/12/50 961,758
Mileage at 9/62 1,578,045
Withdrawn week ending 29/9/62
Scrapped Crewe Works 11/62

6209 PRINCESS BEATRICE at Crewe Works; the date given is 18 August 1935, so we are in at the locomotive's birth. Just visible on the original print, chalked on the smokebox rim, is 'E395 No 7'. The first part is the works reference to the whole batch while 'No 7' denotes the individual engine – 6207 would be the seventh of the batch 6203-6212.

46209 PRINCESS BEATRICE, at the north end of Camden shed, having come off The Shamrock, 20 September 1958. Photograph R.C. Riley.

PRINCESS BEATRICE comes out of a heavy rain shower, in to sunshine, approaching the final cutting that led to Shap Summit. The train is a Liverpool-Glasgow service, near the end of the Lizzies' reign, on 18 August 1960. Photograph Peter Groom.

46210 LADY PATRICIA

Built Crewe
LM 'date built' 6 September 1935
Renumbered 6210 to 46210 week ending 5/6/48

REPAIRS

All Crewe unless
stated otherwise
Figure in brackets
= weekdays out of traffic

4/9/36-25/9/36**LS** (19)	18/9/47-29/10/47**LO** (36)
11/1/37-10/2/37**LO** (27)	3/11/47-21/11/47**NC(Rect)** (17)
17/6/37-28/7/37**LS** (36)	22/4/48-5/6/48**LO** (39)
26/3/38-28/6/38**HG** (80)	10/6/48-14/6/48**NC(Rect)** (4)
10/7/39-27/7/39**LS** (16)	21/2/49-21/3/49**HI** (25)
16/12/39-6/1/40**LO** (18)	15/8/49-12/10/49**LC** (51)
17/6/40-13/7/40**LS** (24)	27/3/50-26/5/50**HG** (51)
7/11/40-19/12/40**HG** (33)	1/12/50-13/1/51**LC** (36)
9/5/41-28/5/41**LO** (17)	12/5/51-15/6/51**HI** (29)
31/7/41-22/8/41**LO** (20)	8/9/51-13/10/51**LC(EO)** (30)
20/12/41-29/1/42**HS** (34)	14/5/52-24/6/52**HI** (35)
30/7/42-7/10/42**HS** (60)	21/8/52-13/9/52**LC(EO)** (20)
11/2/43-10/3/43**LO** (24)	29/12/52-7/3/53**HG** (59)
4/9/43-21/10/43**HG** (41)	6/11/53-11/12/53**LC(EO)** (30)
15/8/44-9/9/44**HS** (23)	25/5/54-29/7/54**HI** (56)
19/5/45-23/6/45**LS** (31)	4/8/55-13/8/55**LC** (8)
28/11/45-29/12/45**LO** (27)	3/11/55-6/1/56**HG** (53)
20/8/46-24/9/46**LS** (31)	26/11/56-4/1/57**LC(EO)** (32)
4/7/47-28/8/47**HG** (48)	16/4/57-25/5/57**HC(EO)** (33)
	25/9/57-28/9/57**NC(EO)** (3)
	13/2/58-29/3/58**HG** (38)
	13/4/58-7/6/58**NC (Rect)(EO)** (47)
	24/8/59-24/10/59**HI** (53)
	20/8/60-19/11/60**HI** (78)

SHEDS

Camden 9/11/35
Crewe North 22/5/43
Western Region 4/2/56
Crewe North 18/2/56
Edge Hill 15/9/56
'Scottish Region' 6/7/58
Carlisle Kingmoor 4/3/61

TENDERS

No	Fitted
9131	6/9/35
9360	25/9/36
9353	16/6/39
9376	20/12/39
9372	13/8/55

MILEAGES

1935	21,857
1936	108,360
1937	71,606
1938	70,716
1939	84,162
1940	66,790
1941	64,667
1942	66,714
1943	49,824
1944	53,811
1945	44,669
1946	64,754
1947	36,520
1948	50,825
1949	49,578
1950	51,826
1951	49,577
1952	56,513
1953	60,988
1954	63,041
1955	60,991
1956	53,386*
1957	58,007
1958	57,430 *'Estimate'*
1959	46,614
1960	43,188
1961	8,830

*'Excludes miles run whilst on
loan to Western Region'
Mileage at 31/12/50 956,679
Mileage at 10/61 1,457,814 – *'does*
not include mileage for year 1958'
Withdrawn week ending 7/10/61
Scrapped Crewe Works 5/62

A blue 46210 LADY PATRICIA, with the characteristic lining showing to particular effect, at Polmadie 6 July 1952. Photograph J.L. Stevenson.

Shame about that post... LADY PATRICIA at Shrewsbury. Photograph B.P. Hoper Collection.

6210 LADY PATRICIA at the Polmadie coaling plant about 1948. The first Pacifics had a strange hot water 'de-sanding' device which washed sand off the rails – see the caption to 6200 at Camden in 1934, early on in the book. On the later Pacifics this device was not fitted, though the sanders remained trickle feed, and in the same position. Quite early on (though the Record Cards do not always give a date) steam sanding was ordered, as seen here. Photograph W. Hermiston, B.P. Hoper Collection.

46210 LADY PATRICIA at Crewe North, 25 July 1952. It would later be one of two Princesses sent to the Western Region when the Kings were withdrawn with bogie defects. Old Oak was the engines' home shed, for a couple of weeks in February in the case of 46210. Photograph J. Robertson, B.P. Hoper Collection.

46211 QUEEN MAUD

Built Crewe
LM 'date built' 18 September 1935
Renumbered 6211 to 46211 week ending 5/6/48

REPAIRS

All Crewe unless	27/5/47-27/6/47**HO** (28)
stated otherwise	28/11/47-6/1/48**HS** (33)
Figure in brackets	15/1/48-12/2/48**LO** (25)
= weekdays out of traffic	7/5/48-1/6/48**LO** (22)
4/5/36-16/5/36**HO** (12)	25/4/49-16/6/49**HG** (46)
6/6/36-29/6/36**LS** (20)	27/6/49-1/7/49**NC** (5)
25/8/36-4/9/36**LO** (10)	23/9/49-30/11/49**LC** (59)
26/12/36-30/1/37**HS** (31)	12/6/50-28/7/50**LC** (40)
2/10/37-27/10/37**HS** (22)	6/11/50-9/12/50**LI** (29)
10/12/37-11/1/38**LO** (27)	17/7/51-21/8/51**LC(EO)** (30)
14/2/38-24/2/38**HO** (10)	21/1/52-28/2/52**LI** (33)
29/9/38-26/10/38**LS** (24)	13/10/52-24/12/52**HG** (62)
22/5/39-8/6/39**LO** (16)	17/6/53-6/7/53**LC(EO)** (16)
6/11/39-23/12/39**HG** (42)	21/10/53-24/11/53**HC** (29)
23/8/40-9/10/40**HS** (41)	13/3/54-14/5/54**LC(EO)** (52)
14/5/41-6/6/41**LS** (17)	2/2/55-9/3/55**HI** (30)
26/12/41-31/1/42**LO** (32)	9/5/55-14/6/55**LC(EO)** (31)
20/7/42-11/8/42**HG** (20)	20/12/55-20/3/56**HG** (76)
16/10/42-31/10/42**LO** (14)	27/6/56-16/8/56**HC(EO)** (43)
17/3/43-7/4/43**LO** (19)	12/6/57-10/8/57**HI** (51)
4/10/43-30/10/43**LS** (24)	17/10/57-23/10/57**NC(EO)** (5)
20/11/43-4/12/43**LO** (13)	5/7/58-12/9/58**HG** (59)
19/4/44-18/5/44**HG** (26)	2/2/59-14/3/59**LC(EO)** (35)
26/4/45-23/5/45**LO** (23)	18/1/60-4/3/60**LI** (40)
30/1/46-9/3/46**LS** (34)	28/5/60-29/6/60**LC(EO)** (27)
12/12/46-18/2/47**HG** (58)	18/7/60-13/8/60**LC(EO)** (23)
	9/9/60-7/10/60**LC(EO)** (24)

SHEDS

Camden 9/11/35
Crewe North (loan) 22/1/38
Camden 26/2/38
Crewe North 22/5/43
Edge Hill 1/10/55
Crewe North 9/6/56
Edge Hill 16/6/56
Crewe North 7/7/56
Edge Hill 29/11/58
Crewe North 7/11/59
Edge Hill 21/11/59
Carnforth 11/3/61
Crewe North 7/61

TENDERS

No	Fitted
9132	18/9/35
9345	29/6/36
9354	5/12/44
9361	4/9/46

MILEAGES

1935	19,043
1936	81,575
1937	76,925
1938	82,457
1939	58,249
1940	73,029
1941	67,886
1942	61,256
1943	58,637
1944	63,891
1945	51,582
1946	52,860
1947	47,894
1948	60,934
1949	48,488
1950	53,579
1951	64,584
1952	46,723
1953	65,801
1954	62,462
1955	62,290
1956	53,219
1957	56,179
1958	59,520
1959	57,959
1960	35,552
1961	14,943

Mileage at 31/12/50 958,283
Mileage at 10/61 1,537,215
Withdrawn week ending 7/10/61
Scrapped Crewe Works 4/62

A tremendous view of 6211 QUEEN MAUD in action on Bushey Troughs, hurtling along with the Royal Scot – about 1936, probably, with its new high sided tender. '500 tons London-Glasgow' looked easy like this! The engine (with 'Caledonian' route indicator...) is heading north on the Down Fast and taking its first water on the journey all the way through to Glasgow Central.

46211 QUEEN MAUD (in what looks like black) at Shrewsbury, about 1952 – note the wonderful signal with three different arms, perched in the station roof. Photograph B.P. Hoper Collection.

Primrose Hill Tunnel provides a perfectly majestic backpiece as 46211 emerges in to the light on an up train, in the middle part of the 1950s.

46211 QUEEN MAUD, with the down Emerald Isle Express, heading away from Rugby on the Trent Valley line, 29 April 1958. Photograph Michael Mensing.

Two Princesses stored at Carnforth, with chimneys 'sacked', 22 June 1961. Behind 46211 is 46203. Photograph Alec Swain, B.P. Hoper Collection.

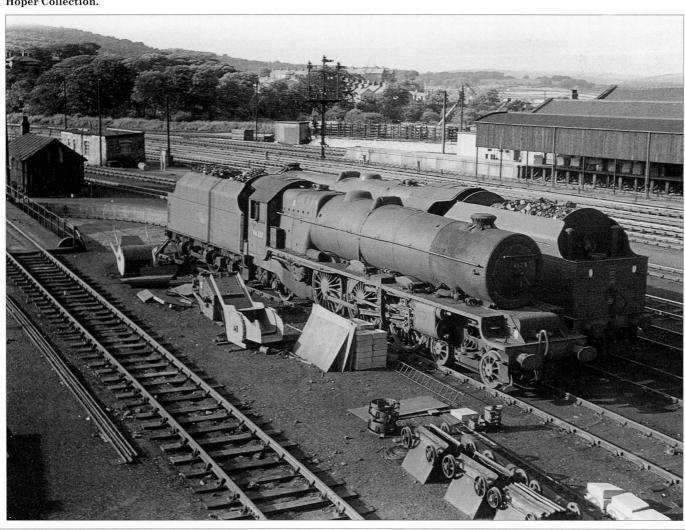

46212 DUCHESS OF KENT

Built Crewe
LM 'date built' 21 October 1935
Renumbered 6212 to 46212 week ending 10/4/48

REPAIRS	
All Crewe unless	8/11/48-20/4/49**HG** (139)
stated otherwise	31/5/49-7/6/49**LC** (7)
Figure in brackets	18/7/49-10/8/49**LC** (21)
= weekdays out of traffic	1/11/49-10/12/49**HC** (30)
7/7/36-28/7/36**HS**	6/2/50-20/3/50**HI** (36)
30/10/36-18/11/36**LO**	27/3/50-20/4/50**NC(Rect)** (20)
9/2/37-22/2/37**LO** (12)	31/1/51-28/2/51**LC** (24)
24/5/37-3/7/37**HG** (36)	10/5/51-5/6/51**LC** (22)
21/10/37-20/11/37**LO** (27)	11/11/51-11/12/51**HI** (25)
16/4/38-26/5/38**LO** (35)	9/2/52-12/3/52**NC** (27)
23/9/38-21/10/38**HS** (25)	25/9/52-26/11/52**HG** (53)
24/7/39-30/8/39**HG** (33)	8/1/53-17/1/53**NC(Rect)(EO)** (8)
7/6/40-29/6/40**LS** (20)	1/2/53-12/2/53**NC(Rect)(EO)** (9)
19/4/41-17/5/41**LS** (25)	20/4/53-16/6/53**LC(EO)** (49)
29/9/41-17/10/41**LO** (17)	17/6/53-27/6/53**NC(EO)** (9)
3/2/42-28/2/42**LS** (23)	1/1/54-25/2/54**HG** (41)
18/7/42-8/8/42**LO** (19)	4/6/54-1/7/54**HC(EO)** (23)
23/11/42-19/12/42**LS** (34)	3/10/55-18/11/55**HI** (40)
4/6/43-13/7/43**HG** (34)	6/3/56-10/4/56**LC(EO)** (29)
23/12/43-26/1/44**LO** (29)	5/6/56-2/7/56**LC(EO)** (23)
23/10/44-9/11/44**LS** (16)	4/3/57-6/4/57**HI** (29)
11/12/44-23/12/44**LO** (18)	7/9/57-12/9/57**NC(EO)** (4)
16/1/45-1/3/45**LO** (39)	6/10/57-9/11/57**LC(EO)** (29)
8/10/45-17/1/46**HG** (87)	5/2/58-15/3/58**HC(EO)** (33)
15/4/46-12/6/46**LO** (50)	1/9/58-12/11/58**HG** (62)
30/6/47-25/9/47**LS** (76)	14/11/58-20/11/58**NC(Rect)(EO)** (5)
10/3/48-10/4/48**LO** (27)	5/4/59-3/6/59**LC(EO)** (50)
	12/11/59-19/1/60**HG** (56)

SHEDS

Camden 26/10/35
Crewe North 16/10/39
Camden 21/10/39
Crewe North 22/5/43
Edge Hill 28/1/56
Crewe North 10/3/56

TENDERS

No	Fitted
9133	21/10/35
9354	28/7/36
9345	5/12/44

MILEAGES

1935	21,295
1936	99,018
1937	69,453
1938	79,001
1939	62,008
1940	69,577
1941	62,202
1942	59,272
1943	57,750
1944	52,171
1945	44,815
1946	48,544
1947	37,353
1948	46,321
1949	35,410
1950	53,440
1951	51,237
1952	58,643
1953	60,160
1954	60,648
1955	60,409
1956	67,373
1957	53,830
1958	53,881
1959	53,817
1960	63,041
1961	5,560

Mileage at 31/12/50 897,630
Mileage at 10/61 1,486,229
Withdrawn week ending 7/10/61
Scrapped Crewe Works 4/62

6212 with original standard type tender, moving away from Carlisle on 14 May 1936. The vehicle behind the engine is the L&Y dynamometer car of 1912, though what tests it might have been going on that day (if any) have not come to light. Photograph H.C. Casserley.

46212 lifts the up Mid-Day Scot past Strawfrank Junction south of Carstairs on the Caley, 21 July 1956. As Allen relates in his book, this was the hardest job undertaken by the Lizzies before the introduction of the Coronations in 1937. They took prodigious loads, not far off the magical '500 tons' of the original estimates and though the train may not have been so heavy in BR days, the Princess Royals, obviously, could take on the jobs of their larger and younger fellows when required. Photograph J. Robertson, B.P. Hoper Collection.

DUCHESS OF KENT busies itself with some shunting at Carstairs, adding vehicles to its train no doubt, for she has express head-lamps. The first two are Western Region SCVs (Special Cattle Vans), then a horse box; the train would be dividing at Carstairs and this is presumably some sort of special livestock movement.

46212 DUCHESS OF KENT on up Mid-Day Scot near Beattock in February 1953. Photograph J.L. Stevenson.

A black-liveried and beautifully lit 46212 DUCHESS OF KENT stands beshadowed at Shrewsbury shed, about 1949. 6212 came out of Crewe in 1935 with an odd 'Derby' throw-back – a smokebox door with a number of 'dogs' around the rim, but this was done away with after some years. Photograph B.P. Hoper Collection.

LIZZIES FROM THE LINESIDE

By Graham Onley

Above and left. Two fine pictures of 46200 THE PRINCESS ROYAL, looking very good indeed at Camden shed at the end of the great day. 1X76 was the up 'Aberdeen Flyer', the special which the RCTS had chartered on 2/3 June 1962, down to Aberdeen on the East Coast with A4s and back to Euston with 46201 and then 46200, and tracked down so assiduously by Onley's Northampton gang. The engine had arrived at Euston 178 minutes late, by which time photographer R.C. Riley had been waiting four hours at Camden shed! The delay was par for the course at that time, with Sunday engineering work on the LNW lines. Were the crew already in the Camden cabin, describing the lunatics, macs flapping, crashing through the allotments somewhere in Lancashire? Photographs R.C. Riley.

If one thing sticks in my mind above all others when I think of the 'Lizzies', it is how infrequently I really came across them. When they did happen along, our mob tended to use the full title of 'Princess Royal', rather than the plebeian 'Prinnie'. Since first hearing the railwayman's 'Lizzie', I have always preferred that term, although the old LMS style of 'a sixty-two hundred' runs it a bit close.

It was probably this scarcity which allowed us originally to refer to them in full, whereas the more common ex-LMS passenger 4-6-0 classes all suffered banal appellations such as Pates, Jubes or Scots – almost as if we had no time to refer to them in proper terms before the next one came along.

Truth to tell, the chance of seeing a Lizzie on our Northampton home patch was only slightly more than not very much! The small size of the class was only part of the problem. The twelve of them (after the tragic loss of 46202) were not, in the main, from obscure, far away places, but from 'local' main line sheds such as Crewe North and Edge Hill, with the occasional Polmadie defectors, though the emphasis, overall, was very much on Crewe North.

The real difficulty was that they only ever seemed to run the more aristocratic main line expresses to or from Liverpool and points north of Crewe, sometimes

reaching Glasgow, and doubtless Perth and Aberdeen on occasion. Those expresses serving Northampton direct, as apart from those scheduled to call at Blisworth with a motor train connection, invariably produced at the very best, rebuilt Scots, which I have to say were very acceptable when set against the otherwise continuous local diet of Stanier Class 5s and 2-8-0s, super Ds and Austerities, garnished with the occasional Crab.

As an aside, it should be noted that Britannias, while eventually regulars on the main line – once 70031-70033 had settled down at Longsight – were also unusual on Northampton line expresses. Only once the whole class had descended onto the Western Division with the 1964 exile and continuing slaughter of the still superior LMS types, could Britannias be seen on literally anything.

The thirteen Lizzies were all running by 1935, but my 'Princess Royal' era was to cover the period from sometime during 1951 until their last days in 1962, or as we will see later, 1963. We all have an era, and I would hazard a guess that most of us consider our own was too late. I often think of what was missed through arriving too late on the scene, or purely through being too young to appreciate what may have unknowingly been witnessed (did I *really* see a streamliner – a main line failure – on Northampton shed?

I am told that I did, so I am tempted to believe it, and I can *nearly* see it in the mind's eye). One has to temper these sombre thoughts with the comfort that those who did manage to arrive much earlier may have missed, among other goodies, British Railways maroon and Brunswick green. These liveries, dare I say, knock pre-nationalisation and many of the garish pre-grouping liveries sideways.

Back to the brutal truth; we could not expect to see a Princess Royal between one visit to the main line proper and the next. Similarly, if we were to manage a sighting at home at Duston West, in Northampton, it was a racing certainty that the working would be a Sunday main line diversion. These diversions were not, during the 1950s, anywhere nearly as frequent as they were to become in the modernisation mania of 1960-1965. It was the seemingly infrequent main line Sunday diversions which forged our squad's view of the typical 1950s Sunday. This was a day of pure tedium, relieved only by the possibility of a new line or two for the ABC after wandering round the shed. A 'namer' was usually too much to hope for, and if one had descended upon the shed, it was most likely in disgrace after a failure somewhere along the nearby main line, at Roade perhaps.

When we did visit the main line at Blisworth, there was still no *certainty* of

The Princesses' long association with Liverpool will be clear from these pages, if only for the number of times they were recorded on The Merseyside Express. All the Lizzies had spells at Edge Hill at one time or another.

a Lizzie – possibly due to the fact that the best chance was the up or down Merseyside Express, and neither of these passed within our parentally-allotted time span.

Prior to mass bike ownership, we had to make do with either the 1.32 or 2.32pm Northampton to Blisworth train, and often managed to miss the down Mid-Day Scot, which passed our idyllic observation point at varying times around 2.00pm. Was our impression of sunshine every time we went to Blisworth something to do with the fact that we were actively discouraged from such excursions during any conditions other than near-heatwave?

Heatwave or not, once we were on station, the loco in charge of the 'Mid-Day' was probably a Coronation or a Lizzie in more or less equal frequency. Once the much-admired 71000 DUKE OF GLOUCESTER arrived on the scene, he took about a third of the action. Admired by the spotters that is, if not by the locomen. It did not take long even for us to get the message that all was not well with the Duke.

Apart from the classes already noted, it should be remembered that almost any other form of double-headed combination could turn up. The thought of an unrebuilt Patriot piloting a rebuilt Scot with about eighteen mixed types and liveries of carriage in tow can still be a mouth-watering diversion during a particularly dreary 1999 meeting, especially if the imaginary Scot had been BLACK WATCH. 46102 seems to have been the target of every young spotter domiciled south of Crewe during my era. Oddly enough, I have no recollection of the classic train combination of two Class 5s run-

ning The Mid-Day Scot, which to me enjoyed an equal status with Royal Scot.

The late on the scene 'Caledonian' was looked upon as a bit of an impostor, a Johnny-come-lately which needed an eight coach restriction in order to make the opposite end of the line in about 6½ hours. I know that Lizzies were very occasionally piloted, but I have no recollection of such an instance, although I have seen the odd photograph.

The loan of 46207 and 46210 along with Coronations 46237 and 46257 to the Western Region, early in 1956 in substitution for ailing Kings had been and gone before junior gang members such as myself even heard of it. This did not necessarily inhibit us on the few occasions we found ourselves in the company of our brothers in arms from the Western Region, usually at Banbury, which by the late 1950s was just about in the range of the more energetic of our squad.

In general, Lizzies managed to keep within the confines of the Western Division. Their size, weight and coupled wheelbase would have had some influence on this, but in addition to the outing on the Western Region the highly popular *Trains Illustrated* – *TI* to most of us – of the time reveals that 46210 ran in both directions over the Waverley route with flood-diverted Beattock route expresses on 29 and 30 October 1954. Likewise, 46211 on the down Royal Scot late in 1959 (unusual in itself) was trumped when QUEEN MAUD found herself diverted over the Settle and Carlisle, due to problems on the West Coast main line proper.

A glance through the shed allocations during my time will show that, until things started to deteriorate after the

end of 1960, most of the class did not stay that long at any shed. If the allocations to Polmadie, at varying periods, of 46200, 46201, 46203 and 46210, are discounted, it would seem that the only establishments to get a look in were Crewe North and Edge Hill, and the continuous shuttling backwards and forwards between the two may have had more to do with the needs of operations, coupled with works attention, rather than the traditional offloading of 'duffers' from shed to unsuspecting shed.

I have always enjoyed a few minutes perusing old 'shed books', and can still be a little jealous of older brothers' teasing, indicating, to the nearest hundred times, how often they saw, say, 5673 KEPPEL. They knew it as an Edge Hill commoner, but to me, it was the unknown 45673 of Perth. Who decided these reallocations? But I digress a little too far...

I admit to not remembering when the last Lizzie was claimed for my ABC. It could not have been much after 1952. I exclude 46202, which never passed my gaze in either of its forms, for we did not consider it to be a true Lizzie. It seemed more of an honourable experiment in its first guise and (from the few photographs I have seen) a visual gem in its second short-lived form – a sort of 75-25 cross between an original non-streamlined Coronation and a Lizzie proper.

Soon, whenever one of 'the twelve' loomed into view, a new entry was not an option, but I never met any fellow enthusiast who had difficulty in bringing himself to gaze long and hard at the elegant lines of whichever lady was passing by. Here I should admit that 46205, with the massive experimental motion bracket

A beautifully turned out blue 46206, pointing north by the 'gonging off' hut at its home shed, Crewe North. Photograph A.G. Ellis, B.P. Hoper Collection.

was, in my humble opinion, slightly less attractive than her eleven relatives.

No, they were never likely to be a catch in the same way as a Jubilee, which to a greater or lesser degree, could have hailed from any one of about thirty sheds, or a Royal Scot. In my days a dozen of the latter came from slightly out of range Holbeck or Polmadie and were, to put it mildly, rare to us. Digressing again, I was even a little disappointed to read recently in our old friend *The Railway Observer* of June 1953, that all the 66A Scots had been seen in London in the first few months of that year. Wherever was I at the time ?

It is easy to slip into the view that the 'fifties was one long period of decline, but that was not the case. Admittedly when the end beckoned, it came fairly quickly, but until the first of the English Electric Type 4 diesels had firmly established themselves, by about the summer of 1960, there was very little change in the overall picture on the local lines. A few Scots and Patriots of the 7P variety had been exiled to the Midland route, but hardly in sufficient numbers for us to notice the loss. The Stanier Pacifics continued in the front line, and when the first diesel-inspired relegations came, the victims were, not surprisingly, the unrebuilt Patriots. These were followed, again not surprisingly, by the Princess Royal class. The Lizzies fairly abruptly found themselves short of the work which had been their main preoccupation since birth. It did not matter that their successors did not exactly excel themselves. Their first stumble into storage was not really that much of a surprise, and it was fully expected that they would rapidly disappear into Crewe Works for their last visit. That at least nine of the twelve

actually returned to traffic for the heaviest part of the 1961 summer was viewed as little short of miraculous by the rank and file. It may be that one or more of the other three (46210, 46211, and 46212) also returned to service, but if so, I failed to see any one of them.

Once the summer 1961 service had ended, the complete withdrawal of the class for scrapping was expected. Even the suggestion that they would be retained for use on fast freight was viewed with scepticism; Lizzies hardly seemed suited for loafing about in marshalling yards with all their trackwork imperfections, and we felt that whoever in authority had THAT idea must have been deluding himself – or did he perhaps have a soft spot for them ?

Many of us probably have our own memories of how we discovered during late January of 1962, the wholly unexpected return to service yet again of a few of those that survived the autumn 1961 cull. That had robbed us of 46204, 46210, 46211 and 46212 in one batch, rapidly followed by 46205 and 46207.

Those returning to service for a second time were 46200, 46201, 46203, 46206, 46208 and 46209, and these ladies certainly had a lot of men chasing them that summer of '62. In view of the fact that the diesels, which should perhaps have performed better than they did, were struggling, we even found ourselves forecasting that a return to store in the autumn of 1962 merely presaged a cavalry-type return during the winter of 1962/63. Had the authorities the slightest inkling of the weather conditions that were in store for much of that well-remembered winter, I venture to suggest that, had they not been formally withdrawn in the autumn, the Princesses

would been back with us some time in January 1963. Yet, perhaps in any event, minimum maintenance during the last weeks of service would have wrecked such a cosy idea.

A few bars of *Telstar* by The Tornadoes forever reminds me that life elsewhere still carried on even as the last of the Lizzies were being withdrawn. Luckily, the same period also saw Northampton Town FC topping, and eventually winning the race for the Division Three title season 1962/63. There was also a minor irritation between the USA and the USSR – something to do with missiles and Cuba.

The nameplates adorning the Lizzies were of the standard LMS type and were, alone of all such plates, to be found on the centre splasher. At a pinch, the Lizzie plates could have been mounted above the leading splasher, though they would have been slightly obscured. Did Stanier instinctively adopt the standard position of his native railway – or did he not have any concern with such details? His apparent lack of interest/enthusiasm for the streamlining of his next Pacifics suggests that nameplate positions would be even lower on his list of priorities. Whatever, I thought they looked fine, and my personal favourites have to be PRINCESS LOUISE and, perhaps a little perversely, DUCHESS OF KENT. I still feel that the double line plates looked far too fussy. Mind, if I was offered one, I suppose I could find a home for it...

Although the chimney suited the balance of the loco very well, the double chimney inflicted on 6201 in its early days looked grotesque, especially when allied to the Fowler-type tender of the early period, and did nothing at all for the lady's looks. That was a sight I am

46206 was withdrawn in November 1962 and like many of its sisters spent long periods stored out of use and wrapped in desultory fashion against the elements. 46206 stood mournfully at the south end of Camden shed In September 1962; the photograph at least provides a useful contrast between the 'coal pusher' tender and the conventional one of another stored Lizzie alongside. The sadly demolished stopblocks were a feature of engine shed life! Photograph D.M. Alexander, B.P. Hoper Collection.

The lineside throng at Lichfield greet a Lizzie (on an up train) with fixed attention (and who can blame them) in July 1955. You did not see them that often, for thirteen – or twelve, rather – was not a great number; take away those at Crewe Works and those on shed somewhere for a night job and they were thinly spread indeed between London, Liverpool, Perth and one or two other extremities of the system. It was not like waiting to see an A4 at Grantham, for instance! Photograph B.P. Hoper Collection.

not sorry to have missed. For me though, the most visually telling aspects were the boiler mountings, and I favoured the style resulting from the rebuilding of the original domeless boilers. The separate dome and top feed, for me, gave a better balance altogether. The oval buffers fitted to the front end really iced the royal cake.

It may have been the great length of the loco (an effect enhanced by that endless boiler) which made it possible to know when one had taken a main line diversion past our spot during absences for meals. My place at the family dinner table put me sympathetically where I could actually see what I was missing (so to speak). The problem was that I was looking across a distance of about two miles as the crow would have flown. But I knew.

Although it may have been necessary to have been a little nearer than two miles away to notice, it should be recorded that two Lizzies, the green Polmadie pair 46201 and 46210, were never fitted with the BR AWS gear. I hope that observation does not render me an irredeemable anorak. If anyone is interested, there exists a photo of Royal Scot 46113 in its last days wearing the early BR emblem on its tender. There is also an earlier one (if the quoted dates are accurate) where it is clearly wearing the later style. I have not noticed such an anomaly amongst the Lizzies, which is not quite the same as saying there wasn't one!

The visual impact of the liveries the ladies wore was often almost lost under the workaday grime, but I can recollect seeing the early BR lined black, probably on 46201. I had no opinion at the time,

but today I would feel that they eventually wore better colours.

The short life of the early 1950s blue was for me tragic; I thought it looked marvellous, but then again I thought the same of the Brunswick green, which, although it is seen as the 'normal' livery, was probably only on all the class at once for the relatively brief period from about mid-1955 to very early in 1958. The surprising arrival of four *maroon* Lizzies was a wonderful touch, which encouraged us to believe that authority actually had a collective heart, and went some way to helping many of us through the last heartbreaking years of the class, with which we had to cope without any form of counselling!

In my time, the tenders had BRITISH RAILWAYS in full, and both versions of the emblem. My vote goes to the emblems over the title, but please do not ask me to decide which emblem is the better.

I even have to confess that, much as I liked the final form of the maroon livery, I fail to recollect (or did I never notice under the dirt?) the earlier lined red, which mirrored that of the green livery.

Most ex-spotters will probably regret that they failed to keep comprehensive records of the engines and trains they saw, on territories at home and away. I am no exception and though my head is full of what I saw, there are few notebooks to go with the memories – so there are few dates, and few actual numbers.

However, during the mid-morning of Friday 21 September 1951, 46207 PRINCESS ARTHUR OF CONNAUGHT entered local folklore as a result of a nasty derailment south of Weedon station, while heading an up Liverpool express.

The reasons for the derailment, in which the locomotive and some of its train plunged down an embankment as it left Stowe Hill tunnel, are well known, and it led to a number of deaths and serious injuries to persons on the train – see the tale of its recovery in this very book. It is an ill-wind, however... and the unexpected bonus for the Northampton spotters was somewhere in the region of sixty hours of main line diversions. With hindsight I suppose the biggest surprise was how well the railway coped with the expresses together with what was then a very heavy freight traffic.

Once the news was out (from the 1.00pm news on the Home Service, to which we listened during our midday break) that afternoon's school became more of a bind than ever, and the 4.15pm finish even more eagerly awaited. Permission had already been given for a later than usual teatime arrival home. The real treat, however, was to be allowed on site at Duston West by 9.00am on the Saturday, when all our wildest dreams were to become reality. I can recollect much of what 'came through', but I cannot recall what became of my comprehensive listings! Nonetheless in my mind's eye, I am still transported back, just one of a crowd of trespassers standing (literally) by the up home signal opposite Duston Junction West signalbox, and gazing up at 46201 (surely in lined black) as it waited for the road with an up express, doubtless on the heels of a freight slogging up towards Roade. I can also still see 46100 ROYAL SCOT in its rebuilt form, crawling up the bank from Northampton Castle station in the wake of 46201 and coming to a stop at the peg in its turn. Later that afternoon, when there must have been fifty of us gathered in the field, an almost new Britannia, which I am almost certain was 70008 BLACK PRINCE, headed south, but via Blisworth, rather than the direct route to Roade. This train we knew as 'the Carlisle stopper' and 70008 (if so it was) would have probably been running in after a little adjustment at Crewe.

After this episode, things so far as Lizzies were concerned settled down into a 'just glad to see one' routine. That is until the delightful re-awakening when, as I have recounted in an earlier *British Railways Illustrated* – BRILL – magazine, a maroon (and admittedly grimy) 46207 had me nearly falling from my cycle at Blisworth in May of 1958. Leafing through the magazines of the period I have realised that, much as I was impressed, the BR maroon livery was, to those who had seen similar events before, just another variation to be taken in the collective stride. Several years of nothing but Brunswick green, which may have been a long period to a youngster such as me, was almost the flickering of an eyelid in the overall scheme of things, following on quickly in the sequence of LMS maroon, LMS black, BR black, BR blue and BR green, leading to BR maroon, all coated and disguised with the familiar layer of dirt, which we almost failed to notice. We sort of 'looked through it' to the engine beneath.

I wrote earlier of seeing 46201 standing at Duston West box. Beyond that, I doubt that I ever saw another Lizzie standing still, except for a few resting on Camden shed, or simmering at the buffers on the arrival side at Euston, during family 'outings' to London to see the sights. I wonder if my parents (and no doubt lots of other parents) ever realised that Camden shed and Euston station WERE the sights of those London outings!

I have no idea when I mutated from a locospotter and became an enthusiast. I am however aware that having been interested in locomotives from the first, they have continued to this day to hold No.1 spot in my affections. Luckily this has not stopped the interest from spilling over into all the other facets of railways which we can now see recalled in minute detail monthly in BRILL.

What I do know is that there would have been pockets of like-minded enthusiasts across the country, spending, like me and mine, nearly all our free time (and often time not belonging to us) as well as most of our meagre income in chasing and photographing anything to do with the passing scene, and incidentally having a whale of a time. The scene unfortunately passed all too quickly.

One of the highlights of this period was what is still reverently referred to as 'the Blackpool trip'. This particular exploit had nothing to do with paddling in the sea, heavy drinking or clambering up the Tower. What it did have was a 1.00am start from Northampton on Sunday 3 June 1962. The Northampton branch of the RCTS had organised a trip by luxury? coach, visiting sheds which were, to me, fabulous names in the early pages of Ian Allan's ABCs and Locoshed Books.

Between landing at Sutton Oak (8G) at 5.15am. and finally crawling, almost literally, round the massive shed-bashing Wembley of Newton Heath (26A) some 12½ hours and fifteen sheds/works later, we had not expected to see even one Stanier Pacific, of either class.

In some ways we were not too disappointed at this, because we had seen and photographed many foreign locos. However, if the date of 3 June 1962 seems familiar to readers, it may well be because it should be. On that weekend of 2 and 3 June, The RCTS/SLS had jointly organised the 'Aberdeen Flyer'. This spectacular special left Kings Cross at

around 9.00am on the Saturday and (please bear in mind that this is memory writing) A4 60022 presided as far as Edinburgh Waverley. Another A4, 60009, took over as far as Aberdeen, where the heroes on board may have had a little time available to do their own thing, which I would bet included visits to both Aberdeen sheds. Or they could have organised their sleeping accommodation while the real intrepids were watching Lizzie 46201 back onto the train for the run back south. At that time of the year, I would imagine that a start of somewhere in the region of 9.00pm would still allow sufficient daylight for photography, but I have not seen many – or any in fact.

46201 eventually reached Carlisle Citadel and handed over the baton to sister Princess 46200, which was to take the train the 300 miles to Euston, and the end of its marathon journey. This last stage probably commenced at about 5.00am on the Sunday morning.

What has this to do with the famous 'Blackpool trip'? It clashed of course with the RCTS 'Head Office' affair (as we might characterise the 'Aberdeen Flyer') and beyond all expectation, some of the on-board Northampton members were destined to see *us* staggering to the lineside, in the wilds of the north west. I was not even a member of the local branch at that time, and having been invited to join the Blackpool expedition (even if only to spread the costs), upbringing made it difficult to refuse the offer made by men who were seen as 'Top Linkers'. To go to Blackpool would mean passing up this late chance to see a Lizzie; the 'Aberdeen Flyer', racing through Northamptonshire behind a Princess would have to be sacrificed.

This, it turned out, did not deter one of our number, who armed himself with various OS maps of the area of Lancashire, and who managed to get various officials at the sheds visited early that

Cheddington (Aylesbury branch to the left) in 1958, and 46207 PRINCESS ARTHUR OF CONNAUGHT roars through with the up Merseyside Express. Photograph K.L. Cook.

46207 PRINCESS ARTHUR OF CONNAUGHT on an up train south of Bushey in the middle 1950s – note PW men in traditional pose...

morning to check (with mysterious calls to local Control) as to the progress of 46200 and its train. I cannot truly remember the timing details, but I do know that by about 7.30am that morning, our coach, as usual a Commer TS3 operated by Wesleys of Stoke Goldington, North Bucks, was running a little low on diesel. Porings over the OS maps, fused with the latest information on 6200's progress required our driver (forever known as CID Sid, but I know not why) to disregard the fuel situation, and acting on orders, he joined in the fun of the chase. When one of the party spotted steam in the cross-country distance, it was a case of *'turn right yes we know its only a dirt track, but keep going'*.

Sid did, and at about 7.45am, somewhere between visits to Springs Branch and Blackpool sheds, and somewhere in open country near Coppull Moor (or so the OS map told us) forty-odd enthusiasts of various ages spilled from the coach, over allotments, past startled gardeners, over through or under the fence, and onto the lineside, just in time to see 46200 storming southwards.

When I contemplate the effort put into that episode by my teetotal friend, it still makes me want to buy him a pint at one of our squad's summer Friday evening get-togethers at the site of Roade station, where such times are pleasantly relived. It is possible that the 'Aberdeen Flyer' was the last ever, possibly the only time ever, that a Lizzie officiated on an enthusiast special. What else were they up to in that last grim summer?

For the summer of 1962, there were just six survivors. Three, 46200 (red),

46201 (green) and 46203 (green) worked from either of the Carlisle sheds, while the other three, 46206 (green), 46208 (red) and 46209 (green), worked from either Crewe North or Camden. During this period, the northern engines all appeared in a very presentable condition, but of those at the southern end of the line, the two green ones could just about be discerned as such, and 46208 might just as well have been a brown tinted grey. The Carlisle engines are reported from various sources as working mainly to Perth, with odd forays south to Crewe, and sometimes even to Euston, not that I saw any of them locally after an appearance by 46203 on the 'Carlisle stopper' on 8 February. The other three seemed to work a combination of expresses from Euston to Wolverhampton, semi-fasts to Rugby, and were sometimes pressed into service on some of the more important trains of the line, such as 46208 on a Liverpool-Euston express on Sunday August 19th. In truth, I felt that their appearances increasingly bore the 'end of the road' look, and I was not wrong.

Once the autumn arrived, with less need for them on the substitutes' bench, withdrawal followed quickly and we thought we had seen the last of them. The only chance of ever setting eyes on a Lizzie again would have to be through the preservation movement. Whatever these amazing people have achieved in the intervening years, it has to be said that in late 1962, they were looked upon as slightly dotty. This did not stop the ultimate preservation of 46201 and for that, we all said thanks. We also thanked Billy Butlin for his efforts with 46203

(and 46100 and a Southern 'Terrier') and felt that we had been very well catered for with two out of the twelve Lizzies likely to last longer than we!

However, all was not *quite* lost. By the spring of 1963 we were all acutely aware that if we did not soon carry out the ultimate aim of every member of our group, that is, to 'do Scotland', it would not be worth thinking about. Accordingly two of us set forth from Northampton Castle late in the evening of Monday 15 July 1963 for 'the trip'.

I must mention that we thought we had seen an unrebuilt Patriot, long withdrawn, dumped in the derelict Preston shed as we passed by in the early hours of the next morning. Other than that, pickings were best described as 'meagre', though a row of withdrawn Jubilees and Scots dumped at Corkerhill provided us with both a major soaking and our first sight of the legendary BLACK WATCH. Not surprisingly, none of these gems carried nameplates, so I have still to see BLACK WATCH, even if I have seen 46102, which was accompanied by 46105, also late of Polmadie.

Eagerly anticipated were the several hours we had allowed ourselves at Carlisle on the homeward journey on Saturday 20 July. I have no recollection of how we made the trip from our 'digs' in one of the city's less salubrious streets, but we eventually found ourselves walking along the 'cinder path that leads to the shed' at Upperby. Our route led past several rows of locos, all obviously dumped and never to turn another wheel in service again. These included a Crab with big St. Rollox type numbers, our first WD

2-10-0, an old-time Midland Division 1952 exile to Kingmoor in the shape of 45640 FROBISHER with both nameplates and St. Rollox numbers and, as the highlight, 46200, still in very presentable condition, though without nameplates.

Needless to say, in the bright sunshine of that Saturday morning, more than a few shots were obtained of the assemblage, and we then happily continued on to find the Foreman's Office; here, it was planned, we would ask for the usual 'look round'. After being thoroughly welcomed throughout Scotland (we had permits for visits, but the times bore little resemblance to the original plans) we were cordially invited to leave Upperby somewhat more quickly then we had arrived. Do you know – we did not care one iota – we had seen a Lizzie when we least expected, and could go home happy.

Below. 46207 PRINCESS ARTHUR OF CONNAUGHT on Camden shed alongside the ash disposal plant. What else but the Merseyside Express? This is the engine chased out to Camden in THE RED REVOLUTION page 61. Photograph J. Robertson, B.P. Hoper Collection.

Above. 46211 QUEEN MAUD with Crewe North shedplate, at Carstairs on 24 July 1954. That's the station in the background, where the Pacific has probably just left the Edinburgh portion of its train. Photograph J. Robertson, B.P. Hoper Collection.

46210 LADY PATRICIA in blue at Polmadie, 26 November 1951. Alongside is a tender of very definite LNER antecedents... Photograph J.L. Stevenson.

'Scene after the derailment of the 8.20a.m. Liverpool-Euston express, LMR, near Weedon on September 21, 1951.' So ran The Railway Gazette's headline - the picture is reproduced from the actual page, so has something of a 'newsprint' look to it, as do others in this section.

Lifting the Lizzie onto the up main line - spectators were allowed onto the down side.

HOW TO RESCUE A PRINCESS

'The locomotive settled easily and with extremely little bounce.'

Raising Princess Arthur.

The derailment of the 8.20am Liverpool-Euston express at Weedon on 21 September 1951 left the train engine, 46207 PRINCESS ARTHUR OF CONNAUGHT, laying on its side at the bottom of the embankment, stuck fast in an English field. How to get it back, and rescue a Princess in distress?

Some excavation of the front of the engine, where it had ploughed itself in to the earth, was done a few days later, for the Inspecting Officer to make an early examination. All the minor debris in the field was cut up and carted off to Wolverton Works in road lorries, in a kind of shuttle service. This relieved the cranes up on the main line of a lot of the work and hastened the time when services could begin again. On 7 October two big accident cranes took away all the rest of the coaches, leaving the engine and tender in the field on their own. Rescuing PRINCESS ARTHUR was another matter; she lay 14ft below the embankment at the lowest point, the embankment itself was soft earth and had already suffered disturbance, the radii for the cranes were poor and a new bogie would have to be put under the engine for transit to Crewe. Moreover, it all had to be done urgently without further damaging any fittings, so that PRINCESS ARTHUR could be weighed and examined by the Board of Trade Inspecting Officer. It was a task to match the most improbable Princess rescue of myth or fairy tale!

The engine was too far out to be lifted direct by the maximum crane power available, Crewe's 50 ton Cowans Sheldon and Willesden's 50 ton Craven and this determined the Motive Power Department on the following plan of campaign:

a) The tender to be rolled up on its wheels and lifted up the bank and rerailed on the down line by cranes standing on the up line. Afterwards, it would be taken to Weedon and stabled.
b) PRINCESS ARTHUR rolled up on its wheels by the same cranes.
c) The engine then to be hauled up a previously prepared 1 in 22 ramp, laid with track. It would be dragged up this ramp to a point alongside the up line where it could be rerailed.
d) In the meantime, the two cranes would run to Heyford, cross over to the down line and take up a position opposite the final position of PRINCESS ARTHUR at the top of the ramp.
e) The tender, with a wagon containing the new bogie, would then be brought on the up line and stabled on the north side clear of the scene. The bogie would be removed by the northernmost crane and placed on the up main line, south of PRINCESS ARTHUR, the tender being held in readiness for coupling to the engine.
f) The cranes would then lift PRINCESS ARTHUR off the ramp and rerail it on the up main line, with the old bogie left behind on the ramp, to be taken away later.

g) Tender and engine would be coupled together and the old bogie placed in the wagon in which the new bogie had arrived, going to Crewe with the rest of the breakdown train.

First of all the bank had to be considerably strengthened by steel piles, wooden baulks and double sleepering on the line where the two cranes would stand. A temporary sleeper platform had to be constructed on to which the engine and tender could be righted.

The two cranes were to be in position by 6am on the morning of 28 October 1951, more than a month after the accident, and the Willesden, Bletchley and Crewe staff canteens put on copious supplies of food and tea. *Five* 8F 2-8-0s would also attend, to act as stabilisers for the cranes and the track. They are labelled A to E on the plans and were also labelled thus in the operation itself; they had to be at specific places at specific times and to avoid confusion carried headboards showing these letters. All preparations, such as packing to avoid shocks to the Pacific's springs, emptying the boiler of water and wedging open the cylinder and steamchest cocks to avoid compression and resistance when PRIN-

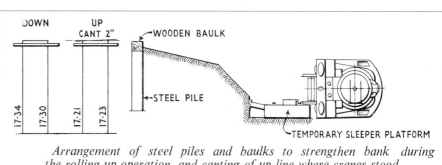

Arrangement of steel piles and baulks to strengthen bank during the rolling up operation, and canting of up line where cranes stood

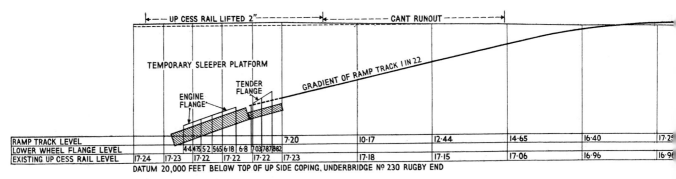

RAMP TRACK LEVEL							7·20	10·17	12·44	14·65	16·40	17·2?
LOWER WHEEL FLANGE LEVEL		4·4	4·7 5·2	5·6 5·8	6·1 8	6·8	7·0 3 7·8 7·8 8 8·2					
EXISTING UP CESS RAIL LEVEL	17·24	17·23	17·22	17·22	17·22	17·23	17·18	17·15	17·06	16·96	16·9?

DATUM 20,000 FEET BELOW TOP OF UP SIDE COPING, UNDERBRIDGE Nº 230 RUGBY END

Details of ramp track up which the locomotive was hauled to top of b...

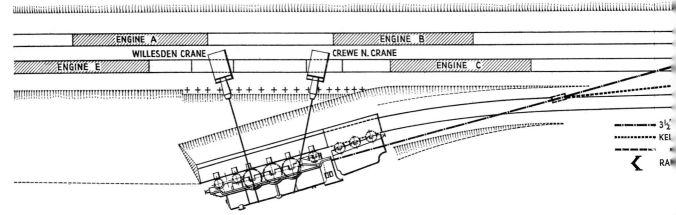

Positions of engines and cranes in readiness for rolling the derailed locomotive o...

CESS ARTHUR was dragged up the ramp were complete by the previous day, 27 October.

Two 8Fs, A and B, were stabled behind the cranes, as close together as possible while still allowing the rear of each crane to swing round while they were engaged in righting the tender. This was rerailed after forty minutes. While this went on, Engine C, which had followed the Crewe crane and train from Weedon, hauled the empty equipment vans back there and stabled them. Once that was done, Engine C coupled up to Engine D (which had remained there) and the two ran back to the site. In the meantime a Kelbus rerailing tackle was hitched up to PRINCESS ARTHUR and fastened to the up main, to act as anchor if the Princess should threaten to run off its platform when it was rolled upright. Engine B then took the tender (in surprisingly good condition) away to Weedon, the engine returning immediately wrong line on the down line to the site.

The cranes had now been manoeuvred and packed to roll up the engine, which was done in much the same way as the tender. Engines A and B once again acted as stabilisers immediately to the rear of the cranes. The Kelbus steel rope anchoring the engine to the up line was now coupled to the drawbar of Engine D and tightened by the engine moving towards Weedon. With the cranes pulling in a carefully orchestrated way, PRINCESS ARTHUR rose up out of the common clay and settled with as much dignity as it could muster on the rails of the sleeper platform: 'The locomotive settled easily and with extremely little bounce.'

The great danger was settling or shifting in the earthworks but the piling did its job and the anxious men with theodolites detected no undue displacement.

Once PRINCESS ARTHUR was upright, an examination was straight away made of the motion, buried in the soil for a month; it had been anticipated that the damage would be severe, and that most of it would have to be stripped down before the engine could move. This was not the case; after the clay and muck had been hosed off and the oil cups and mechanical lubricators replenished, and the piston rod greased, 46207 was ready to go up the ramp...

The Crewe breakdown vans were brought back from Weedon by engines C and D and coupled to the rear of the engine standing on the Crewe crane. Both steam cranes and their trains were now released to go to Heyford as the complicated plan laid down. There they crossed over to the down line and returned to the recovery scene, ready for the rerailing of 46207 on the up line. A complicated arrangement of Kelbus rerailing devices,

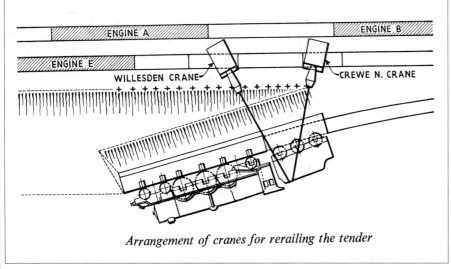

Arrangement of cranes for rerailing the tender

MP TRACK TO BE 5"ABOVE RAIL LEVEL

7·31	17·26	17·21
6·89	16·84	

GINE D

ROPES
ES
KLE

s

together with the 8Fs had been planned, for it had to be assumed that the stricken Princess would be very 'stiff' on its wheels indeed. 46207, however, turned out to be so 'free' after its time in the Northamptonshire mud that it could be hauled with a single Kelbus only, until the Bissel wheel and the first two pairs of coupled wheels were on the chaired track on the improvised ramp. After that it was a question of heaving with a will on the part of 8Fs C and D coupled together, until the Pacific got near the point where it was to be lifted on to the main line. The new bogie had been brought forward from its waiting place at Weedon, together with the tender. The bogie and tender were in place for fitting when 46207 was lifted off the ramp line and on to the main line, and the old bogie was dumped in a wagon. This was half past four in the afternoon; the rescued Princess was given some oil in vital places and then gingerly taken by one of her Handsome 8F Princes the dozen miles to Rugby shed, and Crewe Works the day after that.

The accident took place on 21 September 1951; the engine was rerailed on 28 October and was back at Crewe on the following day, the 29th. Weedon and its fascinating aftermath, however, is not to be found as such in the Record Card, instead 46207 is shown having a Heavy General from 23 September (the Sunday after the accident) until it was ready, a beautiful Princess once more, a few days before Christmas. This is the only time an English field served as an outstation of Crewe Works!

Left. How the Princess was to be hauled up the ramp - it was suprisingly 'free' and a single Kelbus (rather than the two depicted) and a pair of 8Fs, sufficed.
Below . Out of the clay. Some of the 8Fs wait at the top of the temporary ramp. All those weeks and no one pinched the right-hand nameplate!

The Record – Some Notes

The lost Lizzie. The rebuilt 46202, named PRINCESS ANNE, would certainly earn the description 'hybrid' – what Rowledge has called 'in effect a 6ft. 6in. version of the Coronation class'. (The Coronations had 6ft. 9in. wheels.) The kinship with the Coronations is obvious, even to the Coronation-style notch in the boiler – to afford clearance for the lubricator lid – but the old Princess identity reasserts itself towards the rear. 46202 as a reciprocating loco was famous of course, for its short life – eight weeks from leaving Crewe to its terrible end at Harrow on 8 October 1952. This is 46202 a few weeks before, waiting to leave Euston's wooden platform with the 8.30am Liverpool train on 28 August 1952.

Boilers

In previous volumes of this series, boiler changes were shown in each separate works history of the locos. The boiler history of the Princesses is a little more complicated than most, in some ways, however. The 'trail' of each boiler can thus be found separately on pages XX to XX, in the form of the various 'Phases'.

Anything But Not Always Everything

As pointed out in the earlier volumes of this series, *The Book of the Coronations* and *The Book of the Royal Scots*, the LMS Record Cards, while containing much useful and even fascinating information, are a *guide* to what happened to the engines. They are an excellent guide but not an absolutely perfect one; some jobs are given the briefest description, while others, frustratingly, are denoted by a Works Code only. There is always the suspicion of clerical errors, of omission or commission, and aspects of prime importance to us engine pickers – most notably liveries – get no reference whatsoever.

Sheds...

One way or another, the Princess Royal Pacifics worked the London-Perth axis throughout their lives. Rather like the Royal Scots, they thus all spent periods at Crewe North, moving north or south thereof as required, to Camden, Polmadie or wherever. As with all BR steam locomotives, the record fades from about 1959-60 as the people involved realised their charges were on the way out. No one responsible for the Record Cards bothered to record the last 'seeing out mileage' allocations to the Scots, for instance and though this would have been the case with the Princesses they were withdrawn early enough for the 'official' record to match the 'actual' record – that is, late moves as recounted in the railway press of the time match those on the Record Cards.

Works Codes

With one or two exceptions, all repair work on the Princesses was done at Crewe, and while some work must surely have taken place at the sheds, these jobs are hardly ever recorded.

Classification of works jobs also varied over the years and the best we have come up with is: **HG** Heavy General; **NC** Non-Classified; **LS** Light Service and **HS** Heavy Service. These last two evolved by BR times into **LI** Light Intermediate and **HI** Heavy Intermediate. One extra since the days of *The Book of the Coronation Pacifics* is the **(Rect)** which simply means 'rectification' and typically took place a day or two after a major repair – that is, tightening up bits that had come loose and loosening bits that were too tight. They seldom took very long – often only a day. **(EO)** was 'Engine Order', under which some jobs seem to have ordered out of the normal run of things.

The Record Cards represent an unmatched body of endlessly fascinating data, and if the reader gets half as much fun perusing the information as I have had in compiling it, I'll be content.